The Temp
Survival Guide

The Temp Survival Guide

HOW TO PROSPER
AS AN ECONOMIC NOMAD
OF THE NINETIES

Brian Hassett

A Citadel Press Book
Published by Carol Publishing Group

A Citadel Press Book
Published by Carol Publishing Group
Citadel Press is a registered trademark of Carol Communications, Inc.

Editorial, sales and distribution, rights and permissions inquiries should
be addressed to Carol Publishing Group, 120 Enterprise Avenue,
Secaucus, N.J. 07094

In Canada: Canadian Manda Group, One Atlantic Avenue, Suite 105,
Toronto, Ontario M6K 3E7

Carol Publishing Group books may be purchased in bulk at special
discounts for sales promotion, fund-raising, or educational purposes.
Special editions can be created to specifications. For details, contact
Special Sales Department, 120 Enterprise Avenue, Secaucus, N.J. 07094.

Manufactured in the United States of America

10 9 8 7 6 5 4 3 2 1

Library of Congress Cataloging-in-Publication Data

Hassett, Brian.
    The temp survival guide : how to prosper as an economic nomad of
the nineties / Brian Hassett.
       p. cm.
    "A Citadel Press book."
    ISBN 0-8065-1843-X (pbk.)
    1. Temporary employment—United States   I. Title.
HD5854.2.U6H37   1996
650.14—DC20
                                                        96-35585
                                                        CIP

-The Whole Entire Story-

*This book is gratefully dedicated to all women,
for among your number are
my visionary mother Enid who taught me to see,
my first wife Susan who taught by example, and
my lifeline Dawn who taught me I could.*

*And to the great bear spirit, Jerry Garcia,
who's still growlin' in the woods.*

The Temp
Survival Guide

We were interested in everything, as most people are when they're kids before they learn to be automated in a world where you're told your life's function is to put the right fender on the car and do that until you get your pension. And while that's very good in terms of a healthy economy, it's not necessarily good psychically or spiritually for society just to be forced to believe that you can only do one thing and to do that until you drop. The fact that many of us were also trying to be artists, writers, painters, poets, musicians, meant that we were considered by our own families to be certifiably insane. And as a result we had to pull together and share what we'd learned with each other.

—Maestro David Amram, at the Whitney Museum of Art,
New York City, January 31, 1996

1

-A Tempting Life-

Perhaps one of the first questions you have to ask yourself is: "Do I really want to work all that much?" If the answer is "No," you're well on your way to becoming a successful temp.

True Story Department
I remember one night hanging out earning $24 an hour to make small talk with some lawyers at one of America's most prestigious law firms, and all of them were lamenting what they'd done with their lives. They had these huge law school debts, they weren't making diddlysquat in their first years as lawyers, and they were having to work eighty-hour weeks just to stay with the firm. One of them said to me, "I'll bet you're making the most per hour of any of us," and they all laughed until we figured it out, and I was.

Survival in the Post-Employment Age

Technology is changing our economic world like speed dial channel-surfing. We're flying through changes in seconds that used to evolve over centuries, and it's only getting faster. The era of "forty

years and a watch" died with Rockwell, and I'll bet there's even some of you who aren't sure who Rockwell was.

Whether you're being forced into temping by an economic downturn, or you're looking to supplement your current income, or you're an artist or student who needs part-time funds to fund the full-time dream, temping will change your life. It's fun, flexible, lucrative, empowering, experience-building, skill-enhancing, cash-flowing, plus→

Temps Are Cool

Temps answer to no one. We're like the nomadic circus workers of the Wild West, the Woody Guthrie train hoppers, the woolly menace Dennis Hoppers, the secret spies who slip under cover of the night. People don't even know our names. We don't ever have to be anywhere, or do anything, and that's the way things are going to stay.

Temping will expand the flight pattern of your migrations. No longer will you be walking the same road to the same factory to work with the same people until the lights go out. As an autonomous free human at the crest of the millennium, you're in a world of geographic freedom where laptops and cellphones are taking you places your grandparents couldn't even imagine. And now your skills are about to take you even further!

Tuition-Free College

Every temping assignment is like a trip to the United Nations, a Berkeley philosophy class, or an M.I.T. computer lab. It's an opportunity to meet and work with people from the widest spectrum of our communities. In fact, one of temping's greatest rewards is the rainbow collage of cultures you're exposed to. Each day you have an eight-hour time frame to explore your new universe. You can use this tuition-free seminar in life to understand the Haitian mother's troubles with her two teenage boys, or ask the

4

Born Again how you can get to heaven if you've already sinned and plan to again, or the Egyptian if she considers herself black or white, or the computer guy about the fastest way to the root of your program.

Temping is a paid college education, except every day's a field trip and there's no homework! You get to take an extended safari through the fields of human interaction, constantly testing and improving yourself as you go. For the rest of your life you can practice getting along with people until you get really good at it. You can master the old Make-This-Person-My-Best-Friend-in-the-Whole-World-Before-Noon routine. You can treat each day like a new test of your computer skills. Or your secretarial skills. Or whatever quality you want to improve each day. And did I mention the pay?

Stop Worrying About Money

The part about not knowing where you're going to be tomorrow or whether you'll get work next week scares some people. First of all, you'll get work, I guarantee it. Follow these easy-to-read instructions and I'll make you rich or at least give you the confidence to find your bliss career, or help you live more and work less—so stop worrying about money. You'll have plenty. In fact, if you want, you can make more than you ever have in your life, so chill out. It isn't the money, but what you'll discover along the way that makes this so interesting.

SURFING GENERAL'S WARNING: Lots of people aren't cut out for surfing the waves of uncertainty, and I don't want to suggest that you dive in unless you're okay with letting them take you. If you want to have a safe and particular view of the ocean, stay on the shore and homestead some beachfront—there's nothing wrong with it. It's safe, it's steady, and you can string up some party lanterns.

This is really the quandary you're facing:

What am I going to do with my life?

You're wasting valuable time thinking, "I'm completely screwed up, aren't I? Look how low I've sunk! I'm actually reading a book about *How to be a Temp*. What's next? *How to Miss a Bus?*"

So-called "average" people retiring today have worked in 4.7 different jobs in their lifetime, according to the Office of Randomly Selected Numbers—but now you can do that in a week! Assuming we get only one shot at life, wouldn't it be better to have done more than 4.7 different things by the end of it?

Most people feel scared to leave their regular job for a variety of financial and psychological reasons. One of the most common is "If I sit in this chair long enough, eventually I'll be promoted and be able to sit in a more comfortable chair and hate my life a little less."

Temping keeps the future open. You can move when you don't like the neighbors. You can stay home and work on your own projects, or go to the park when nobody's there—any time of the year. You work when you want and don't when you don't. *You're a temp!*

The Most Lucrative Job-Search Program in the World

Besides everything else, temping is also the most lucrative job-search program in the world. In fact, all sorts of studies of employment patterns have found that people get higher-paying jobs after first working as a temp. So, not only does it pay you to look for a job, but you'll get a bigger paycheck when you're hired!

Later on I'll include an entire chapter on going full-time, but the essence of it is that temping switches the balance of power in the salary negotiations. You're no longer hat-in-hand hoping for any kind of a job, but rather confidently employed by various temp agencies and making more money than you ever have in your life, so this new potential employer better be offering something pretty special to lure you away from where you're already quite happy, thank you. In fact, one of the causes of the boom in the temping business has been the failure rate of employment-hiring practices. The story goes something like this:

The Temporary Times

Today: Sunny and Warm   50¢

NEW YORK—Back in the old days when a beetle was just an insect, a business would hang a HELP WANTED sign in its window, or if there were a lot of jobs they'd go hog-wild and take out an ad in the local paper. The people who applied were mostly what they seemed and probably knew somebody who knew the boss, and if they didn't smell too much like beer at the time, they got the job. Then the beetles became the Beatles and the whole world went to pot, so to speak. Inventions were patented, industries grew, leisure time became Big Time, and with the globalization of television, people became stupider.

This didn't become a problem until we actually had to go to work the next day and the poor employers had the unenviable task of hiring the TV Generation. Even as they became more careful in the selection process they still ended up with a roomful of Ralphs and Potsies. The only thing they could do was to try to make the testing process more thorough, perhaps follow up on a reference now and again, and have several people involved in the decision-making. Except it still turned out after only a few short weeks that the TV nobs they hired couldn't spell their vegetables and thought Murphy Brown was a real person.

And thus, the temporary world was born!

Know What You're Working Into

If you've ever had a job, chances are the impression you had at the interview bore little resemblance to your daily reality. As a temp, you get to actually do the job and make your decision after having worked there. Imagine if they let you move into a house before you decided to buy. Or you got to wake up with your date the next morning before first going to bed with him. That's why temping's so great: You get paid for having breakfast instead of getting screwed at night.

Now, rather than spending your days getting all gussied up and trudging from interview to interview following phony ads while losing money on parking, lunch, and clothes—you get *paid* to go in to a company that needs extra help, so you can interview *them* for a change. And at the same time you'll be collecting contacts, expanding your resumé, and learning new skills. You are suddenly freed up to float above the employment surface to see where your piece fits in the giant jigsaw puzzle of life.

Tell your agencies you're interested in specific fields so while they're keeping you working at rent-paying assignments they can also be looking to place you in your dream job. Registering with the right agency can catapult you over the wall into the middle of the profession you seek. Once you're inside it's up to you to hustle the gig (at which point, turn to the "Landing a Job in a Day" chapter).

By working somewhere, you're distinguishing yourself from the stack of resumés in the pile because not only will the company know who you are, they'll have the chance to evaluate you on the job. And you have the chance to shine. They see you, you see them, and whether you mate for life or it's a one-day stand, you still get paid for the time you're there. Plus you're spending the day on the inside of your profession where the bulk of the jobs are created and filled.

If a job, like an apartment, makes it into the classified ad pages, there's probably something wrong with it. I've gone on plenty of temp assignments at prestigious companies you'd think from their reputation were really nice, but once you got on the inside they were petty or dirty or stodgy or cheap. If you only saw their personnel office when you interviewed, you might have ended up working there. As a temp, you'll never have to go on another unpaid job interview again.

Living When Other People Aren't

One of the best areas to specialize in is off-hours work. This is a huge benefit of the temping biz that rarely gets mentioned, so it's a good candidate for your own personal capitalization.

Regular Joannie

Commutes twice a day on crowded roadways or trains, then runs her errands after work in the crowded store before it closes, then goes to the crowded park on Saturday with everybody else in the world who's trying to get away from it all, so by Saturday night she just gives up and gets bombed, then wakes up Sunday morning and joins a TV ministry in Florida.

You and Me

We sleep in and do whatever we want all day, including shopping when the stores and streets are empty, or having the museums and parks to ourselves all day long. If we feel like it, maybe around 4 P.M. we can call in for work, then while everybody else is clogging the other side of the road leaving work, we cut over to the empty lane and arrive at a place where everyone is already pooped from slogging through a full day's flogging—but we're arriving with the joy of being alive and just in time to make those extra dineros at the evening rate. After a little cushy nighttime work including a free three-course meal and being sent home in a car with enough leftovers to feed a family of four, we stay up as late as we want doing whatever we want until sunrise because we have nowhere to be tomorrow, such as work.

Sex and Where to Get It

Let's face it, one of the safest places to meet that special person is on the job. Everyone's putting their best foot forward, even shy people can find excuses to talk to people they like, and you all get off around happy hour.

By taking jobs in different positions in different parts of town, you quickly begin to see which ones offer the best type of people in your preferred demographic.

You know how you're always thinking about the same few prospects where you work now? And you keep coming back to: your first and second choices are taken, and three and four aren't even really worth talking about. Then you run through the rest of the possibilities and you're down to the Fed-Ex guy, or the girl in the elevator last week. No wonder!

How about this: Every day, for the rest of your life, you get to go to a different almost foreign location with a bunch of new people, except they're all from your hometown, and they're actually quite a lot like you, and you go there for eight, ten, twelve hours at a time, mingle, maybe have a little lunch, chat on the phone, meet over coffee, share a desk, share a job, share the sidewalk at the end of the day 'n' date in the sunset dusk as you walk together from the mirror and glass palace into the twilight's last gleaming. How much would you pay for this kind of romantic adventure? $100? $200?

What if we paid *you*, that's right, YOU, to go on this dating spree! Don Pardo, tell her what she's won! "All right, Dave: You'll be taking home the financial security through regular temping to keep yourself independent, beautiful, and free, well into the new millennium. Plus, you'll receive a lifetime supply of cute prospects *who've got a job* parading past your desk like models on a runway until you take your pick!"

Yes, that's right! In the Dream Come True, Am I Reading This Right? Wait a Minute, I Think I'm Getting It Department:

Go to your phone right now. Dial 1-800-MyAgent and they'll have you wrapped in a bun warmer faster than you can say Calvin Klein.

Actors and Writers Alert

One last thing for you actors, writers, and artists that's even more profitable than the rates: on each assignment you're stationed smack dab in the middle of other people's lives for a day and get to study all different kinds of characters, and then leave! It's like being a taxi driver or a waiter or something, except for the high pay I may have mentioned and the fact you're sitting in front of a computer.

There you are, quietly writing your novel, memoir, or screenplay, minding your own business and appearing to be working so that after a few minutes the other people around you don't even know you're there and begin going about their very strange business. And people are extremely weird if left to their own devices, believe me.

You get to study successful executive bosses and how they got that way, or the most efficient secretaries and how they do their work. In fact, I've learned every desk organizing trick in the entire world (and you'll find most of them in chapter 8).

Back when you first started at the job you're currently at, you probably learned ways of doing things from the people there—from accomplishing their goals to ordering a delivery. Wouldn't you be better off if you got to work with and observe *thousands* of people a year rather than the ten or twenty who work in one place? As a professional temp, you're actually paid each day to add new colorful characters to an ever-expanding palette.

But enough of this. Let's start making money.

2

-The Way the Business Works-

"Work cures everything."
—Henri Matisse, 1953

Temporary employment agencies work by recruiting a pool of workers ("temps") who they can then send out on jobs ("assignments") when a company ("client") needs to fill a position ("got it?").

Agencies earn an hourly rate from the client the way you earn an hourly rate from the agency. Usually the agency is charging the client half again what they are paying you, although this varies among agencies and cities. If you earn $5 an hour, the agency will bill the client $7.50 an hour, so they'll earn $2.50 for every $5 you earn. If you earn $10 an hour, the agency will bill the client $15 an hour. If you earn $18 an hour, the agency is billing the client around $27 an hour for your services! That's over $200 a day!!

The number of clients the agency's salespeople can win over; plus the number of new temps they can secure through recruiting, referrals, and advertising; plus the number of responsible workers they can retain through good counseling and other benefits, equals the success of the agency.

You are an important part of that equation. According to a recent survey by *Tempdigest* magazine, the greatest challenge facing temp agencies is recruiting new employees. This means—advantage *you!* They need you to stay in business, and you're doing them a favor by choosing them over all the other agencies actively trying to recruit you. And you can surf. There's no exclusivity in this business. Agencies know the best temps play for many teams.

When an agency sends you to a company for the day, you *do not* work for the company in whose office you find yourself. No matter where you go on the job, *you always work for the agency.* If you walk out on a job, you are walking out on the agency.

As a temp, you are not entitled to the benefits and perks of the places you get sent. You may receive all sorts of food, tickets, and other freebies, but it's only what they may want to give you the day you're there. You're entitled to nothing. This can feel a little awkward when there are company parties or candies that get passed to everyone but you, but remember: They may get a free candy cane every Christmas, but you get a life. All fifty-two weeks are yours, with the option to renew.

If you take a permanent job with a company that an agency sent you to within six months or a year of temping there, the company is required by law to pay your agency a fee. (Read the back of your timesheet for your agency's terms and conditions.) (Don't think this isn't important just because it's in parentheses and sounds like legal something-or-other, because it really is important to read the contractual laws that both you and the client are entering into by signing the timesheet.) (It's very interesting.) (The way people avoid legal fine print.)

This no-hiring clause is to protect agencies from losing all their good temps—whom they've spent time and money to recruit, test, and sometimes train—to the first job they go on. And it prevents employers from using temp agencies as a fee-free job-search program.

If you try to circumvent this and get caught, you end your relationship with the agency, plus lose them as a reference, and the company is subject to legal action, which is usually a cash settlement, of which you get none.

I'm not a real stickler for rules, but this is one area where it's not a good idea to break the law.

If you're put in the position where a client wants to hire you but is not willing to pay the agency a fee, talk to your counselor. If you are straight about the situation, the agency can call the company and if the company still isn't willing to pay a fee, they can work something out, such as a deal where you would temp three months and then go permanent without a fee. That way everybody wins: You get the job, the agency gets a three-month booking, and the company gets the employee they want.

Rates and Shifts

If ever the Theory of It's-All-Relativity applied, it's in the pay rates of temp jobs. The same word processing skills that would earn $5 an hour in a college town during the school months in the daytime could pay $40 an hour on weekends at a New York law firm. There's no point in giving you hard numbers; you'll discover your local rates yourself in the first three or four calls to agencies in your area.

The first, or day, shift is from 8 or 9 A.M. to about 5 or 6 P.M.; the second, or evening, shift is from 5 or 6 P.M. to midnight; the third, or graveyard, shift is from midnight to 8 or 9 A.M.

And they pay in that order, too. Your evening rate should be 10–20 percent higher per hour than your day rate. And the graveyard rate is 10–20 percent higher than the evening rate. Do not accept less.

If you're uncertain as to what your rate is, at the first agency you go in to, quote high. If you don't know whether you should be getting $5 or $15 an hour, tell them $15. Quoting high is the only way to ensure that you'll get there. If you quote low, they'll never voluntarily move you up the scale. If you quote high, the agent can come back with, "We usually pay people at your skill level around $X per hour," and then you know the standard rate. They won't think badly of you if you quote high, so go ahead and try. Also, if there's any flexibility in the range (which there almost always is), the agent will offer you the higher amount if she thinks you're looking for more.

Once you've quoted high at a couple of agencies and heard their rate-of-the-month response, you'll have the empirical data to base your future negotiations on. What they are quoting you right off the bat is the lowest you'll ever be paid. From there you can play that rate off all other agencies and you'll be sure to always maintain that minimum. Once you get a dollar more somewhere else, every other agency has to match that or you'll work exclusively with the one that's paying you what you're worth.

Thirty-three Hours a Day

True Story Department

As a keen way to illustrate shifts and rates, as well as to give you an idea of the fun ahead, I remember back in the days of long nights and Heineken lights, that fateful spring morning I answered a call to Greed & Avarice, the fancy law firm I'd been courting with my disastrous ways. I was supposed to report to a fellow Irishman named Kelly. He was one of those gangly lawyers whose arms seemed to reach out of his suit as if he'd outgrown it on the way to work. He was real nice and had that pale white skin that evolved over the centuries of hiding from the English by standing still in the fog.

We met at 9 A.M., making this a "day" shift, when the rates are the lowest and the phones are the busiest. Most temp assignments begin during the day. But they don't all have to end that way.

Around 5 P.M. it was obvious that not all the work was done so I asked if he might like me to stay for a little while, figuring I'd pull in a couple more hours since I was already there, and he was appreciative of the offer. At 5 P.M. I had completed a regular eight-hour shift and thus began an "evening" overtime extra shift, with a 20 percent raise in pay, and a 75 percent chance of free food.

The deal was "closing" tomorrow (see chapter 8, "Closings and Candy Bars") and Kelly was the honest kind of man who wouldn't rest until everything was right. To add spice to the night, he was also a fellow leprechaun, so we were both able to fly around the office invisibly and spread Good Luck dust on unsuspecting chairs. By the time midnight rolled around, it was obvious we weren't going to have everything done, so I volunteered to stick around and earn another round of Heinekens.

Beginning at midnight, after seven hours at the evening rate, I got buried in a "graveyard" or "night" shift, the third different rate and shift of the day, with another 20 percent hike per hour and the guarantee I'd be put in a car to go home. This gave me a second wind. When I called and ordered us an exotic breakfast with fresh-squeezed orange juice as a sunrise surprise, you could feel the third wind rising.

As the other attorneys began arriving in the morning to start looking over the four-leaf clovers we'd been working over all night, it became obvious no other temp could pick up the fiddle and dance the jig this late in the gig, so I dug down and thought, "What's the big? If I can keep going for three days in a row on the weekends, why can't I do it when I'm being paid?" I was swayed. So I stayed.

Now I was all the way back where I started—at the regular 9 A.M. day shift—except I could claim the round-the-clock exception, continuing to collect the night rate even though it was back to being the "day" time. You should have seen the looks on the other secretaries I'd greeted the morning before in the same clothes. They'd gone home at five, done God-knows-what till God-knows-when, had a nice long sleep, commuted back to work for day two of their flogging, and I was still working away in the same position they'd left me yesterday. Great double-takes. But I digress.

So there I was making a million bucks an hour and feeling like I was hardly being tested but everyone was being mondo-sympathetic, so I just played the old Marie Antoinette routine and had people fetching me cake and coffee all day. In fact, I sort of became a zoo attraction.

People would parade by in front of me to see if I was real, and then I'd suddenly move really quick and scare them.

You can probably guess what happened next. That's right. They shipped me to Washington to mate with Ling-Ling, the giant panda. But not before I could begin yet another shift! At 5 P.M. on the second day after I arrived, I began my fifth consecutive shift, which would have been an evening rate if I had been a normal person and not a bear.

Finally at 6 P.M., after I'd earned approximately enough money to purchase the firm, they shoved me in a limousine with a bottle of champagne, a box of chocolate four-leaf clovers, and my thirty-three-hour Olympic endurance medal—one for every revolution on my turntable.

The Over-Forty Guarantee

Any employee who works over forty hours for the same agency during the same one-week pay period is entitled to overtime pay of time-and-a-half for all those hours worked over forty, according to the Fair Labor Standards Act of the United States. Agencies will try any number of methods to get around this—such as not mentioning it to you—but all are required by federal law to pay you your rate, plus 50 percent more, for every hour worked over forty.

When calling/faxing/mailing in your hours for the week, mention to the payroll department how many hours are over forty and that they are time-and-a-half so that you let payroll know that you know. There are no exceptions to this rule. No matter how many different clients you worked for, as long as you were employed by the same agency, you are required by law to be paid time-and-a-half. Don't accept less. If you ever have any problems with this, first talk to your counselor at the agency about it. If you don't get satisfaction, tell her supervisor. If you don't get the money, contact one of the numerous government agencies that enforce these laws, many of which are listed in the back under "Official Places and Secret Numbers." Temp agencies really hate to be investigated by the U.S. Department of Labor.

Always Get Paid

If you're sent by an agency to a job and get fired, or the client decides they don't like your work and are not going to pay the agency for your services, the agency is still required by law to pay you for all your hours. You are paid to work, not necessarily do good work. The agency must pay you if you're where you are supposed to be when you're supposed to be there. However, if you ever take a job that goes badly and the client is so upset that they're refusing to pay, if they have a legitimate grievance, you may want to consider waiving your wage for the day and call it a learning experience.

Some small-time clients try to get out of paying their bills this way. You'll be the only person who truly knows the truth in this situation. The agency will hear two sides—yours and the client's—and won't know what really happened. If you honestly screwed up and you force the agency to pay you, which you have every legal right to do, it may be a while before that agency sends you out again. If you really put in an honest day and you did a lot of work and you suspect the client is just trying to skip out on a bill, stand up for yourself. Tell your agent straight-up and directly that you did everything that was asked of you, the work got accomplished, the conditions were not as stated, there were obstacles created by the client, and perhaps this guy is just trying to gyp both of you out of your fair wage. Agents are pretty good judges of character since they do it all day and all year. If you are in the right, they'll know from the tone of your voice. Which is how they'll also know if you're lying.

Transportation

On most jobs it's customary to provide transportation home after dark. Most employers routinely provide either a car voucher, taxi slip, or extra hour of time to pay for door-to-door car service. This is necessary because the companies that have evening and graveyard shifts often work until an hour not on regular bus schedules.

Ask about transportation before being sent out on a job. When the client is desperate for you to come in they'll agree to anything (like paying your way to or from work). Once you're there they couldn't care if you walked home on your knees. *Do not* accept jobs that will not pay for your transportation home after whatever hour you consider safe. Things happen to people and no stupid temp job is worth nightmares. We're in the dream business here.

Types of Temps

The more areas of specialty you can learn, the faster you'll be called for work in general because the agency has a feeling you can handle anything. Temping is a fair, open-minded, open-ended profession in that way: there are a lot of different types of skills to be learned and you can pick any one of them to try and be good at. It doesn't matter if you're a man or a woman, or what your race is, or even how good-looking you are. If you're proficient at Quark or can read lawyers' scribble you can join their ranks and make their money. Learn a skill, milk a cow. You're just a temp. Moo, man, moo.

Many people are unsure as to the hierarchy of the anarchy, so in an on-going effort to promote harmony I'll hum a few lines of "Oh, the Temps I've Known."

The rates will vary depending on where you live, what you do, and the time of day. As you're aware, the value of skills fluctuates based on supply and demand. Just ask a blacksmith. As sure as the campfire crackles, the first one now will later be last, because the times are always changin' in Templand.

To give you some sort of basic frame of rate reference, I'll cite prices in effect in New York City at one fixed point in time so you can see the relative differences between the levels and how much you might be gaining by learning a new skill or program. These rates are for comparison purposes only. Do not try to replicate them at home. New York rates are stratospheric compared to anywhere else in the country due to the high cost of living and the low chance of survival.

Building Web Sites

All shifts: $28–$50 an hour. The newest entry in the computer sweepstakes—not many people know how to do it, so it's the highest paying. The way agencies test applicants is for you to give the agency your own Web page address, or examples of ones you've built. Then the agencies call them up from their office and assess your skill level. If you don't have a Web home page, you can provide splash pages of your work. Splash pages are the flashy logo front cover pages that show off the design and list the options. Even though more and more industries are going on-line, not many people currently know how to set up sites. If you have the skills, register with more agencies because some are getting more job orders than they can fill.

Help Desk

Day shift: $22–26. Evening shift: $28–30. Another entire area of temping that most people aren't aware of. Applicable for any major program. You become a phone support person for the day, like one of those 800-number help people. Not only must your skill and communication level be high, but you must be patient with frantic people since this is the 911 of cyberspace.

Graphics

Day $15–25. Evening $20–30. Also known as desktop publishing or animation operators. Both Mac and P.C. In fact, pretty well all skills are applicable to both formats. Graphics operators are usually required to have more years of experience on the job front. Whereas using Microsoft Word to write your papers for school can get you started as a word processor, making your own comic books at home won't qualify you for a graphics assignment. Agencies require one to five years experience as a professional in the field before they'll send you out to a client on a deadline. The graphics temps are known to be hip and colorful. So if you are one, you are one. "Programs, programs, can't tell your paychecks without your programs." Graphics programs include all versions of the following: Quark Xpress, Adobe Illustrator, Premiere, Photoshop, PageMaker, PowerPoint, Persuasion, Harvard Graphics, and Lotus Freelance. General animation programs include Visio and Macromedia Director.

After this level of high-paying, high-tech expertise we drop out of the computer stratosphere into regular word processing jobs.

Word Processing Centers
Day: $17–19. Evening: $19–23. Graveyard: $21–24. This is the peak of word processing operators. You must test at 70–80+ words-per-minute typing in order to qualify, as well as be a resident expert at the program in question. And Centers are where the most work is done, as in typing all the time you're there. If this is something you're into, Center work may be for you. If you would rather preserve your fingers for later in life, you may not want to follow the central path. Center work pays more per hour because you're supposed to be unstumpable and should know every command in your program. The advantage is you're usually stationed in a separate area from the rest of the office, there may be a more relaxed dress code, some funky tunes, a little doobie smoking, a cooler of cold ones, a blender with margarita mix, shot glasses and strippers. Downside: Usually no windows.

Legal Secretary, Executive Secretary
Day: $16–18. Evening: $19–23. Graveyard: $21–24. Legal secretaries are the partners in the law firm of secretaries. You must be letter-perfect in your execution. If you make a

mistake you get bumped down to regular old word processor. This is like the All-Star game for secretaries, except the points count. It's like a championship flapjack bake-off out in the woods somewhere except, well, you're sitting in a lawyer's office typing. It's, like, really hard, but then once you get used to it it's, like, really easy. It's a good field to pursue if you're anal retentive and detail-oriented. People who understand the vital importance of typing out the entire state name on an envelope instead of using an abbreviation may find a home in the legal secretarial ranks. These are the bowing penguin maitre d's of the office staff, the high-priced boot-lickers of the computer literati, the desk-polishing Felix Ungers of the document crunching crowd. It's a skill you have to work your way up to, but if you have it, the pay and working conditions are in general superior to run-of-the-mill office-hopping word processors. Executives are out of the office a lot. Lawyers are on the phone a lot. There's plenty of downtime. In fact, this book was written during executives' lunches and lawyers' conference calls. Not only is there such thing as a free lunch, soon you'll be getting paid for them! And I'm sure you're thinking, "Now that I could do." Just be sure you can cover the "letter-perfect" part. It's not a knowledge of the law that's required for legal secretaries so much as an understanding that instructions are not general guidelines, and that wording is not approximate. If you want to make it to legal secretary, you need to prove to your agent that you're flawless in other high-pressure word processing situations. You have to show a little style and have pinpoint accuracy in such programs as Microsoft Word for Windows, WordPerfect, SoftSolutions, and CompareRite.

Brokerage, Financial, Investment Banking
Day: $16–18. Evening: $19–22. Graveyard: $21–24. This and legal are the big two in the House of Temping. The

Tom Hanks and Sharon Stone of Temptation. The Stone Temping Pilots of the 747 cash flow. The added zero on the end of your paycheck.

True Story Department

On this one job for some investment bankers at a Major International Bank, all I did for months, was order them lunch at 11:25 A.M. Oh, and I'd stand around the table as the delivery guys laid it out and then nod when they were finished. It's hard to imagine how all those Savings & Loans went under. Oh, the joys of banking! The work is boring. But the people, surprisingly, are not. Maybe they're looking at spreadsheets for breakfast, but they make sure to have fun when there's downtime or they run the risk of becoming disgruntled.

Bilingual Word Processors

Day: $17–19. Mostly day shifts. If you speak a second language, inform your counselor immediately. As more and more business goes global, multilingual word processing requests are increasing every year, especially for Spanish and Russian. If you used to be fairly fluent in some language, query your counselor on how much work there is in it and decide if it's worth boning up.

Regular Word Processors

Day: $15–17. No evening or graveyard without specialty skills and experience in legal, brokerage, or Centers. Examples of money-making word processing and other programs are WordPerfect 5.1 and higher, Lotus (WordPerfect and Lotus is a good combo), Paradox, Microsoft Word for Windows, and Excel (Word for Windows with Excel and/or PowerPoint is another in-demand combo). This is the basis of the temping business, "where it all started," the middle of the bell curve where the bulk of the jobs are. At this level you might be sent anywhere from a small business with a dust-covered computer in the corner to try and get out a special mailing on their shaky dot matrix printer balanced on a folding TV-dinner table to a giant corporation where you'll be dwarfed by stacks of paper in a roomful of uniformed midgets. Once you prove to the agency (and yourself) that you can handle the different situations presented in the word processing world, you're open to other temporary options. But this is the basic prerequisite program you must safely complete before becoming a legal or brokerage operator.

Medical-Hospital Word Processing Specialist
Day: $12–17. It's the same rate as general word processors even though it's an area of specialty, mainly because hospitals don't pay the high salaries that the vital professions such as brokerage services do. This is good for people who enjoy helping other people, and it's a way for medical students, nurses, or anyone else connected with the profession to be a part of it, network, and learn more by tapping their database. There's a lot of regular work in this field because hospitals just don't have enough regular staff. Nursing itself has become a niche in the temping industry, so the same agency could get you work in two different areas at the same hospital.

Entertainment-Advertising Word Processing Specialist
Day: $14–16. It pays less because it can. People will work in fun places for less money. For a few dollars more an hour you can work in boring places with people in suits. Drop your rate a few dollars and you'll be in more creative, interesting environments that might lead to something more. Again, it will depend on your relationship with your counselor and agency as to how much work in this area you get. These are desirable jobs and they're easy for the agent to fill. It's another reason to go the extra mile on other assignments and win brownie

points because later they can reward you by sending you to MTV for a week. You should never tell your agency this is the only kind of work you want, because unless they're an agency specializing in this field, you won't get enough work to stay alive, and the agencies don't think too highly of temps who aren't flexible. Every major city has agencies specializing in each of the areas listed here. If working in one field is your primary goal, be direct about it on your first round of interviews and phone calls to agencies by asking how much of their work is in the field you're interested in. Following your bliss is good advice, but always remember to plant some seeds where the potatoes grow so you're sure there's always food on the table.

Publishing Word Processing Specialist

Day: $13–15. This is even further down the financial ladder than entertainment. As author Ken Kesey put it, "Anybody who's been associated with the publishing industry knows money moves through it very slowly. Everybody likes to get a hold of it and hold on to it as long as possible because they're usually making a little money off it in other places." Notoriously low-paying, like teaching, you have to do it because you love it. Because many people who type also write, and many people who write want to be published, there's already a huddle of word processing writer-types hanging around the lobby with manuscripts under their arms waiting to go in and work for free if they could just maybe leave their novel behind. You must be clear with your counselor if you want this kind of work because if you're registered with the agency at a higher rate of pay, you'll be passed over for these jobs. This is like any other word processing assignment, except the conditions may be a little shabbier, the work load heavier, and the rate level lower. But you'll overhear more interesting conversations, meet curious people, and probably leave with a free book or three.

Proofreader

Day: $12–14. Evening: $14–17. Graveyard: $16–18. This is in the Going Blind Department, and I don't know how these people do it—but it pays fairly well, you don't have to know how to type, and there's often a lot of downtime. It's pretty much prevalent only in the fields of law, finance, and publishing, so it's a good way to get in the door of these different fields.

Paralegal

Day: $10–12. This is not something that you would want to do with, say, your life. You should consider becoming a paralegal if you enjoy leaving the office on hundred-degree days, taking public transportation to some old municipal warehouse of a courthouse, and sitting in a giant echoing room with tiles falling from the ceiling and no air conditioning but plenty of sleeping homeless people, convicts, lawyers, and other unsavory types waiting in creaking pew after reeking pew with everyone in serial-killer moods as they mumble in their own distinctive way about wanting to hear their name called somewhere before the end of time. Which, after two or three people have been carted off dead and your name is finally read, is always followed by the classic civil servants' commandment, "I'm sorry, I can't help you. You're in the wrong room. You need to go to Room 27C in the west wing. This is the east wing."

P.C. Input (a.k.a. Junior Secretary)

Day: $8–12. Must have basic word processing knowledge. Must be well spoken and have good English skills because telephones are often crucial here. As the skill requirements drop off in these lower job categories, applicants should compensate by being stronger in other areas, such as demeanor, politeness, articulation, and appearance. If you have some skills but are unsure of yourself or if your typing speed is slow, this is an area where you can break in with little risk. The client is not asking for a wiz-bang operator so they won't be pressuring you to do anything more than very basic word processing. You'll be able to test the waters of the market and see if you're above or below this basic level, or you can use it to train yourself for a few months before working your way up to the higher-paying but more demanding jobs. One of the Secrets of Temping is that a lot of the most interesting and memorable jobs are in this category because it's the small quirky businesses that usually hire temps at the lower rates.

Data Entry

Day: $7–9. Can range anywhere from boring to really boring. Skills Required: None. Enjoyment Factor: None. Rewards: None. Chance I'd Do This Again: None. These are the kinds of jobs you take when you're really desperate and the job market is dead or you have no skills and you need to get out of the house for a while. You'll get to enjoy your days keying in responses to a survey filled out in pencil on newsprint by two-year-olds in each of seventy-four different fields—and there are only forty more crates of responses to do.

Guy/Gal Friday (a.k.a. General Office Assistant)

Day: $7–9. Big Bonus: No skills required! Entry level position! If you can't do this, you may as well become a paralegal! About all you need—which, sadly, eliminates so many—is good English, common sense, and basic intelligence. Some light typing, light phones, and a light lunch characterizes a Guy/Gal Friday day. This is really the break-in job where you can get work to gain experience and be part of a good agency with the ability to learn computer programs. You can also get yourself an agent who will be looking out for you and can help guide your way up the ladder. It's also a really interesting and *underrated alternative for noncomputer temps.*

No two days as a Guy/Gal Friday are remotely the same. Half the time you're going to glitzy corporate offices to help answer phones, move boxes, or serve new clients champagne, and the other half you're going to the house of someone who runs some sort of small business, usually rather unsuccessfully or else they wouldn't be hiring you as their entire fleet of employees.

Guy/Gal Fridays have the greatest leeway for memorable weirdness of any of temping's categories, as in some little old lady who runs her own mail-order greeting card business out of a labyrinthian apartment where she leads you down a dark, narrow passageway stacked high with dusty cardboard boxes and furniture and books piled over your head, past room after dark room and hallway after endless hallway leading off to blackness. Clothes are hanging from ropes that are strung all over the ceiling like a net, with the bottoms of shirts and skirts brushing against your hair like cobwebs, until you finally get to a little room in the core center of her night gallery, with one yellow lampshade illuminating her myriad collections. She wants you to put some labels on envelopes because she can't peel them with her fingers anymore, but first she wonders if you'd like a fresh muffin. After she brings it with a glass of unasked-for milk and places them on a shelf you hadn't noticed, she sits down in a chair that seems to wrap around her like a giant pillow as she asks you where you're from. Hours later she shows you the greeting cards and they're each a handmade original piece of art.

Receptionist

Day: $7–9. If all else fails, you can always just sit there. Many a great temp got his or her start at the reception desk. You'll usually be required to handle multiline phones with anywhere from 5 to 100 lines, but what self-respecting

American hasn't juggled that many calls on a Saturday night? Also, you'll be expected to have a good speaking voice, know how to transfer calls, use intercoms, take accurate messages, sometimes set up conference calls, and not get frazzled easily. The secret to the reception bay is that it usually has a typewriter upon which the ambitious can practice their typing to get their speed up to where they test higher at the agency and can start climbing the ladder you just read all the way down to the bottom of.

Temporary Alternatives

It's good to know that although half the work in the temp business is secretarial, the other half isn't. While you're waiting for the score on your typing test to improve, here are a few alternative temp jobs that might keep the cash flow flowing: accountants, balloon inflators, bartenders, bus boys, butlers, car counters, chauffeurs, chefs, clowns, costume wearers, dental hygienists, hamburger flippers, house cleaners, movie extras, musicians, nurses, party greeters, Ross Perot signature gatherers, sandwich board wearers, sign painters, subscription sellers, telephone fund-raisers, ticket brokers, truck drivers, or waiters.

And if there's nothing on that list you can do, you can always run for Congress.

To let you know how diverse it gets, there was a friend of mine who in the course of a few weeks was sent to a mall dressed as a bag of popcorn, a baby beauty contest to be a judge, all the video stores in town to see if they were displaying a particular poster, and a real estate auction to show the properties.

Life is by no means confined to an office. In fact, the alternatives to regular temping are the reason some people regularly temp. The offbeat, the bizarre, the twist of temporary fate that can land you as an extra in a Stevie Wonder video, or giving away frisbees at the beach, or passing out free drinks at a garden party are but a sampling of the civic duties a citizen of Templand is required to perform. And the kicker to the whole phenomenon is you get a check in the mail in a week!

This kind of free-association temping can lead to stronger relationships with your agents by showing them you're flexible and can perform well in a variety of situations, plus it gives you the chance to collect some rave reviews while bringing home enough free stuff to fill your house. There are always going to be some temps who don't feel comfortable dressing up as different types of food, so agencies are always looking out for the snap, crackle, and poppers who don't mind a little adventure in their cereal. If you consider yourself more of a Variety-Pak than a Family-Size, you may be catching a lot of free meals at the Temporary Diner.

Obviously there's no way to prepare for such unique and ever-changing experiences, except to sign up at an agency and start working. So let's get started *right now!* Here's how the whole thing works:

How You Get a Job

Sally the Secretary gets sick and calls her supervisor's voice mail and says, "Hack, hack, I'm sick." Her supervisor comes in between 7:30 and 9:00 A.M., hears the voice mail, and says, "Yeah, right," then calls the temp agency. The temp agency then tries to find a temp (maybe *you!*) to sit in Sally's seat.

So basically where you *don't* want to work is at a temp agency in the morning. There's just a blizzard of phone calls coming in: temps with their availability, new registrants calling about signing up, and companies calling to request temps. And speaking of blizzards, you can turn to "Blizzards, Flu Season, and Other Highlights of Temping," for more on getting the most out of every season.

But I fear this is all happening too fast. Before we go any further let's be sure we've totally covered→

3

-Your First Steps-

The standards in temping are so low, if you've read this far you're already in the top half of the class. I go into jobs late, hung over to the point I literally fall asleep at my desk, do absolutely no work the entire day, and at 5:00 they say, "You're the best temp we've ever had. Can we have your name for next time?" As long as you can keep your eyes open and breathe at the same time, you'll be running your own agency in no time.

Here are a few additional skills that may help in some situations: typing, speaking English, and knowing a computer program designed in the last ten years.

On the off chance you think you can do this sort of thing, here are the basic steps of the routine:

Typing

You have to be able to type, the faster the better. If you can't type, forget it. Learn to type, practice, play, have fun on your keyboard and everywhere else. If you're one of those people who absolutely loathes typing and has to hunt for the Q key, then the secretarial office computer temping world may not be for you.

For the rest of you, practice and get good at what you do, do it at work, do it at home, do it wherever your spirit should roam. Get your errors down and your speed up. Most temp agencies will send you out if you score a minimum of forty words-per-minute with five errors or less on their typing test. The store that sold you this book will also sell typing books. Buy one. Or go to a library and borrow one. It only takes a couple of days, maybe weeks. Practice. Go further. Live longer.

At your interview, the agency will have you type some tricky letter for five minutes, then they look at how many words you typed and divide by five, and that's how many words you type per minute. Test yourself (because if you can't test yourself—who can you test?) Top temps and secretaries clock in at 100–120 words-per-minute on a computer with less than five errors, but 40–60 w.p.m. is plenty and will have you temping in no time.

Common Sense

It's odd to have to say it, but the essential quality that most temp agents say they're looking for is common sense. All other skills and shortcomings can be compensated for, but not this one.

Temping sometimes seems like the real world in that common sense is the lubrication of survival, the blood that surges through your every action. If you don't have common sense, you're like the lone cow that wanders into the river and stands there till he drowns. You're like the poodle that barks at the German shepherd. No, wait...you're not that bad.

Common sense is the most common kind of sense, but that doesn't mean everyone's got it. There are many successful people who don't have common sense. Hugh Grant, Darryl Strawberry, and Marion Barry immediately leap to mind. Very happening people, but lacking the kind of common sense that tells you if you're smoking crack with hookers in a seedy motel room while you're still, technically, the mayor, you should probably check the flower pot for cameras. That simply savvy gene is missing in more people than you'd think. In fact, sometimes it seems like there's a world shortage of sense, and it's driving the price up. If you've got any in the attic, it may be worth more than you think. Throughout these pages we'll try to figure out the best way for you to make as much money from it as possible.

I've made Common Sense a separate section in order to show my spiritual affinity with the great Thomas "Window" Paine who wrote, "These Are the Times (That Try Men's Souls)," and many other popular protest songs of the '70s, and also to draw attention to its value and importance. It's such a simple thing: "Oh, by the way, use your brain." But so many people don't. By using yours you can set yourself apart from a large segment of your competition. We can talk about computers and typing speed and networking and all the other grooming techniques to make you as effective a job-surfer as possible, but one area that can push you up entire pay levels is your proficiency in common sense. It's something you gain through a little hard work, like muscles, and the more you practice, the stronger you get.

Vocabulary

It's sad but true—people do judge you by the words you use.

Obviously language improvement applies first to people for whom English is a second language. But they know they need help and are already involved in an ongoing language development program just by being here.

This is for those of you for whom English is your first language and who still have a problem.

Because of increased telecommunications, your voice more than appearance or body odor is a principal factor in hiring and, obviously, determining your worth as a human being. Employment agencies all across the country are reporting a continuous drop in the language skills of applicants. Since most of the jobs placed through agencies involve some level of interacting with other people—such as customers of the client—you're expected to speak clearly and intelligently. This seems to be harder and harder for young people to do these days as the gap widens between the language of the streets and of the business world.

Once again, this is an area where you can distinguish yourself. Knowing that standards are low and dropping like a cinderblock off an overpass, be sure to always keep your language skills at the highest possible torqueage and you'll distinguish yourself from the metalheads.

If you have any doubts about the pronunciation and clarity of your speech, there are many voice and diction classes, schools, and programs in every city in the country. Look in your Yellow Pages under "speech." Look in your soul under "help." If you feel you have any kind of lapse in this area, you need to work on it right away. No matter what you do you're going to have to talk to people.

If you have doubts about your vocabulary, there are many self-help books, tapes, and programs that will gladly teach you very little in exchange for all your ready cash, or you can just change your reading habits. You'll already be changing your working habits by temping. It's what we read plus who we listen to that equals our vocabulary. Change the radio station you listen to. Change the TV shows. The people you talk to. Ask the meaning of words you don't know. Listen for the new ones. Use them.

Flip open a dictionary for once. In fact, have one sitting open on the desk of your work area; don't have it closed on a shelf because it's too hard to pull down and start flipping through. If it's already sitting open on the desk, your eye can just glance over to the columns of definitions smiling in your face and ready for freeform flippage.

In fact, I'll go so far as to say go out and buy a new dictionary. What year's your last one? The good ones cost around $50 but they'll last you for most of your life and change it, too. In fact, I'll even recommend the *American Heritage College* edition. It's the one with the pictures in the margins which we used to pooh-pooh back in our snobby English major days when words were propped up as reverential icons instead of being fun toys we could break. I like the pictures. In fact, it makes it hard to look up a word because you always get distracted by some intriguing image as you're flipping through. And when was the last time a dictionary was so much fun you couldn't stop reading it?

English is the greatest of all English inventions, and we keep improving it every year. In fact, it's growing so fast that words that once took generations to make their way into the language now weave into the fabric and leave again within minutes. As English solidifies itself in the global market via the tube and the Web, regional words are uploaded into its rich stream from cultures on six continents.

Language isn't something you have; it's something you do.

Computers

You have to be conversant with, and preferably enjoy, computers. If you don't, temping may not be for you.

One of the exciting and wonderful things about temping is that you get to try all these different computers and keep up on the latest trends in technology without ever buying a thing. The places where you'll be working will often have the newest, most happening computers, monitors, keyboards, and programs and you'll get to be a test pilot without ever buying the plane.

Computer programs change by the hour. Plus, each company can modify their systems to suit their needs so the same keystroke in one company may not do the same thing at the next. There are two rails to this track and you have to have a wheel on both.

All *aboooard!*

First

Pick one program and master it—work in it all the time, tell a few tales in it, do your Christmas cards, your recipe file, anything. Just use it, play with it, twist it, make up tasks to do like creating a database of your friends' addresses just so you can try to merge files, etc. By learning one program's functions all the way through to the end you'll understand how all programs work. Which leads to the other track:

Second

Play with and learn other programs. Here's why: Computers and their programs will forever be changing. Even though some programs linger on for years, no version of any program will ever last because they're just like leaves on the trees: there's new growth every year, and the old ones just fall away. So don't get too attached to any one program and figure you're home free for life. Learning to work on a computer is like learning to drive a car: just because you learn on one make and model doesn't mean you can't drive others. They've just got the gear shift in a different place and the radio stations set to different channels, but you can still drive them. Don't be scared to try. Fear of computer adaptability is numero uno on the limitation charts for novice operators. Therefore, expansion on this track is the easiest way to distinguish yourself from the rest.

There are lots of ways to learn new programs for free. All agencies have computers in their offices to train on. Ask your counselor when the slowest time is and schedule yourself to go in and learn a program. All programs offer introductory tutorials that take you step-by-step through them at your own speed.

With the advent of Windows technology, most of the jobs you go to will have several programs installed on their computers. While you're there, switch to another program and run the tutorial, or just make your own test file and start trying to do things using the program's help key when stuck.

You don't learn to drive a car by reading a book, nor can you learn a computer that way. Books spell out the laws, but the only way you really learn is to sit in the driver's seat. One job's worth a thousand words. So if you'd just start working I could write a much shorter book.

Tools

I thought I'd mention some of the tools to put in your pack before we set off in search of the giant yet somehow elusive Cash Cow.

The Telephone

I recommend AT&T and no other brand. I don't know if it's their hundreds of years in the business or what, but they definitely make the most durable home phone units. I've personally dropped mine from considerable heights more often than I want to admit and it keeps on ringing. The model you buy should come with a ringer switch that allows you to turn the ringer off while allowing your personal secretary (or "answering machine") to take calls without disturbing you. This feature allows you to freely tell the overnight staff at your agencies to call you anytime because you can turn the ringer off when you're sleeping. Also, the phone should have at least twenty speed dial lines so you can program in each of your agencies as well as your favorite people. Imagine: If this tip gets you one day's work it's paid for the phone.

A typical scenario: You don't know if you want to get up in the morning so you put the phone by your bed and set the alarm; without even opening your eyes you feel for the agencies' pre-set speed dial buttons and, beedleebeep, it's ringing your agency. You don't have to look up the number, you don't have to think about whether you want to call them, in fact you don't even have to wake up. Imagine the happy happy joy joy of setting your alarm for 8 A.M., staying asleep, but still managing to call your top agencies, saying your name, telling them that you're available today, then going back to your blissful dream-adventure with nary a blip. You're only going to actually be woken up if they call you back with work. If you can find another profession where you can get work without even opening your eyes, e-mail TempNation@aol.com about it. Also— and I know I'm going on about the telephone, but it's how you'll make all your money for the rest of your life—deposit the extra nickel and get the deluxe hummer which also has a speakerphone. If you don't have a speakerphone at home you're temp lite. How many times are you on hold a week? Millions. While you're sitting there holding the receiver listening to that android woman's voice about the nine options you can choose, I just hit the speakerphone button and carry on about my business until I hear an actual humanoid. It also means you can fake that you're a big TV executive if you ever need to, which by chapter 8 or 9 may be an option. I also recommend the very visual LED (light emitting diode) read-out screen and digital clock. This too pays for itself within a month because all your calls begin clicking away like a rigged taxi meter. You'll immediately notice your long distance bills dropping because you won't be chattering away for as many minutes with this damn clock staring down your every natter. Obviously cordless phones can't provide all these recommended features, so you need to go to a phone center to get one of those twenty-five-foot twisty receiver cords *and* a twenty-five-foot phone cord to connect the unit to your wall jack. This is the most important unit in your house. Treat it with honor, respect, and a spritz of Fantastik when dirty.

Call Waiting

A necessity, not an option. Although 85 percent of you already have it, you're starting off in the bottom 15 percent of the class if you don't, and you may as well just suck your thumb and take a nap. If it gets you one day's work it pays for itself for the year. If a counselor at an agency gets a busy signal once, she will think your phone's out of order. If she gets it twice, she'll think you are.

Phone Answering Machine

Use this instead of a call answering service for the primary reason that you can't screen your calls with those automated phone service systems, and selecting who you talk to and when is one of the keys to successful anything. You have to be available twenty-four hours a day, but you have to be able to avoid people, too. Just like at a summer cabin, screens are essential for keeping the bugs out.

Screens
There are five color-coded levels to this screening process and they'll all be on the midterm, so start memorizing. Condition White

means the ringer is on and the phone machine is turned off, so if someone calls you have no defenses up whatsoever and are wide open to telemarketers and other unsolicited sleazeballs who should collectively be put on a very large boat with nothing to play with but an intercom system and shoved off into the ocean together forever. Condition Green means the ringer is still on so you know when someone's calling, but the phone machine is also on with the volume up, so you have the choice to pick it up or let it ring through to the machine to hear who's leaving you a message and then decide whether to pick up or not. Yellow is the caution condition; you've now turned the ringer off so you no longer have the option to pick up the phone when it's ringing but must wait until you hear a voice coming out of nowhere in your apartment and just before you think you're crazy because your mother is speaking to you right here in the middle of your apartment one thousand miles from home, you see the yellow light and realize it's only a screen. Yellow is still the most popular coverage level in the world today, and is especially effective for people trying to avoid those nasty Wrong-way Feldman dates who just won't let a bad thing go. And just as a little support for Colonel Mustard's color in Clue, I'd like to point out that yellow was also Van Gogh's favorite color, Corazon Aquino's color for her peaceful revolution in the Philippines, the color that children draw sunlight, and on those psychological tests that measure a color's effect on the brain they've found that yellow makes you feel tranquil and at peace, which dovetails nicely with not answering your phone. You see? It's all quite simple. Condition Red, of course, means Stop! in the name of love. The ringer is off and the volume is down so you neither hear the phone ring nor the voice inside your room when the machine clicks on. This condition allows you to continue about your dreams in peace while your electronic secretary takes messages. Condition Black means black-out; the ringer is off and so is the machine. You are as totally shut off from the world as you would be at one of those expensive spa retreats, except this didn't cost you a dime and you still have all the comforts of home. And now, because I want you to do well on the midterm, here's what to write on your sleeve:

White	Ringer on	Machine off
Green	Ringer on	Machine on, volume up
Yellow	Ringer off	Machine on, volume up
Red	Ringer off	Machine on, volume down
Black	Ringer off	Machine off

(Copy and put beside your phone machine!)

Beepers

The pros and cons of getting a beeper, as first articulated in Shakespeare's *Homey:*

> To beep or not to beep: that is the question;
> Whether 'tis costlier in the end to suffer
> The slings and arrows of missing an outrageous fortune,
> Or to take a credit card against your sea of competition,
> And by buying a beeper, beat them. To shop: to buy;
> No money; but with that charge card to say we end
> The heartache of missed work, and the thousand natural
>   shocks
> That losing money causes, 'tis a consummation
> Devoutly to be wish'd. To buy, to sleep;
> To sleep in: perchance to dream: aye, there's the fun;
> For in that lazy morning slumber what dreams may come,
> When we have shuffled off our full-time jobs,
> Must give us pause: there's the freedom
> That makes temping so fine a life;
> For who would bear the whips and scorns of unwanted
>   salesmen,
> The numbers wrong, the proud man's wakening,
> The rings of despis'd ex-lovers, the laws of Murphy,
> The insolence of offices calling when we sleep,
> And the spurns that patient temps must take,
> When he himself might his quiet make
> With but a turned-off beeper?
> For who would grunt and sweat under a weary life,

But for the dread of something after work,
The undiscover'd retirement country from whose border
No traveler returns, puzzles the will,
And makes us rather bear those beeps we hear
Than miss the jobs we know not of?
Thus beepers do make workers of us all,
And thus the native hue of resistance
Is sicklied o'er with the regular beeps for work,
And gigs of great pitch and moment
With but a beeper their currents turn our way
And lose the name of unemployment.

Beeper costs vary, but in most cities you should be able to buy a cheaper beeper for under $100. Then you have to hook up with a basic service which you can do for less than $10 a month in most urban areas. Beepers aren't a necessity, but they pay for themselves because your counselors know they can reach you instantly—so they use them. Imagine this: The job order comes into the agency at a time when everyone is busy trying to fill other jobs. Is the counselor going to take the time to dial the number of someone who's sometimes home—or someone who *always* answers their beeper within seconds no matter where they are? Now you can be faster than a speed dial. More powerful than a Pentium processor. Able to leap into tall office buildings in a single phone call. It's Supertemp! Mild-mannered secretary by day, Supertemp flies on a moment's notice to any assignment, fighting off the evil competition and inserting indented bullets, all in the name of truth, justice, and the American way of working overtime.

E-Mail and the Internet

This has nothing directly to do with getting temp work, but it's so interactive and fun I just had to mention it. If you aren't on-line, call America Online and get on right now. It costs $9.95 a month and will get you started. AOL is kind of like the McDonald's of the Internet, but you have to learn to eat somewhere. If you want to get on-line and get a free start-up disk and fifteen free hours to explore for a thirty-day trial period, call AOL to hook you up and tell them Karmacoupe sent ya. 800-827-6364.

Business Cards

Have them made right away. As a temp, or a permanent job hunter, you'll be coming in contact with a lot of people in the next year. All the cards have to say is your name, address, and phone number (plus fax and e-mail if applicable). By having cards with just your name, address, and phone number you can use them until you move. This is another one of those If-it-gets-you-one-day's-work-it's-paid-for-itself things. And it's also required equipment in most fields of battle. You can't be regarded as a serious contender if you can't say, "Here's my card." And the first time you say that, you'll thank me.

Daily Planner

Indispensable to life as we know it. If you already use one, you'll have identified your favorite style, whether it's the little pocket-sized ones, the larger one-page one-day books, or the 8½″ × 11″ weekly planners. Whatever your preference, this will be your Bible, map, munitions stash, and first-aid kit for your tour of duty. It should have your agencies listed in it, as well as all your friends and other personal numbers. This allows you to adjust your scheduling on the fly because you may get asked at the end of a day to stay the night, or at the end of the week to come back the next. You need your contact numbers with you to change upcoming commitments. Without a traveling datebook you risk losing thousands of dollars a year. And if the planner helps with some non-business social/dating benefits, who's to argue? I recommend the (Week) "At-A-Glance" brand professional appointment books. Even though the seven-day week is the most illogical of all the man-made time units, it's the unit of time that most applies to the temping/employment world. You're often booked on a week-by-week basis, and it's easiest to evaluate your schedule when your next seven days are visible in a single open-page spread. Also, they have flexible covers and a special ringed binder system that allows you to fold the cover around backward.

History of Your Life

The other crucially vital element to keeping a daily planner is that at the end of the year you have an accurate record of your movements. If it has a black cover, as with the "At-A-Glance" series, use white-out on the spine to paint the last two numbers of the year. If it's a light color use a big thick black felt pen to mark the year. Then put it on your bookshelf near your desk at home. Then buy the same brand every year and repeat the process, including marking the spine in the same place each year. In no time, well, actually several years from now, you'll have your own personal time-life library of your own notes regarding your own life, including such memorable moments as where you worked, the social appointments you wrote down, your concerts, dates, trips, and all your yearly behind-the-scenes phone numbers, contacts, and jobs. But remember—this offer is not sold in stores. You can't buy it for any price, but you can get it here for free. If you ever need to know what you did at a particular time in your life, now you'll have a rough draft dialogue between your history and yourself.

Notepads

You can buy them by the box or bundle in any major stationery store. Don't bother buying them one at a time. I recommend stiff cardboard backs because you can use them as clipboards; white paper because yellow looks sick; 8½" × 11" because legal size doesn't fit in anything; narrow-ruled because it gives you more space per page; and a nice firm binding, preferably with perforation. These will be used simultaneously to evaluate different agencies, one pad per agency, so you'll need a bunch. You'll see. Other things too. Very important. Go buy.

Sidebag

Or briefcase, large purse, or knapsack. I don't think you should arrive empty-handed after all the trouble they've gone to to put together the company and all. As you'll soon read, I've got more plans for you than Napoleon had for Europe, so you might want a little something to tote your treasures in. May I recommend a nice sidebag in black, perhaps an over-the-shoulder style approximately the size of your daily planner which could also hold all your pens, projects, prospects, and perfumes, because life is uncertain—but you don't have to be.

Computer

Obviously it's not essential to have your own computer at home, but it's good for business. Familiarity and ease of operation around a keyboard and mouse are quickly recognized at agencies and job sites. If you are *not* comfortable on a computer that's all the more reason to get one. Using it at home for pleasure—whether playing games, surfing the Internet, working with graphics programs, or just writing letters—is essential to gaining a high comfort level with the units that most of your contemporaries use. If a new computer is not in your price range, there's a glut in the used computer market as more and more people are upgrading and trading in their old models. Look in your Yellow Pages or the classified pages of your local paper. Any basic unit from the original "P.C." on up is going to give a novice the opportunity to advance one whole rate bracket. K'ching!

Fax Machine

Not essential, but now that they're under $200, why not? Many agencies require signed timesheets to be faxed in. Since you don't get the timesheet signed until the end of the day when it's usually too late to borrow the client's fax machine, which shouldn't be your first choice anyway, by having one at home you can send in your hours at all hours and not have to depend on Kinko's.

Watch

Need one. Know travel time for next time. Know how long to go each day. Know when to call. Know time.

Map

You're going to be going to all sorts of new places in the city you thought you knew so well. Hopefully you don't already spend all your time around skyscraper alley or the industrial parks, so these temping locations should be unfamiliar to you. The faster and more precise you are in learning and adapting to your new environments, the more you'll maximize the experience of making money. Immediately acquire the most recent maps for the public transportation in your area. Due to the temporary world we live in, routes and times are changing so fast that last year's map might be just that.

Bike

Especially if you live anywhere there's a flat surface. Not for all people and all seasons, but depending on your location it's very likely a bike could get you there as quickly as any other mode. It's free, doesn't get stuck in traffic, skirts train delays, trains your skirt legs, strokes your cardio, and puts color in your cheeks. Ed Begley does it. Oprah does it. I do it. You do it.

Rollerblades

I don't know if these will directly get you temp work, but you'll make more money by living longer and get more dates 'cause you look better. Work isn't everything.

Appearance

In order to blend into a corporate office environment, you've got to dress the part. You must have at least one week's worth of office-style clothes.

For guys that only requires one tie (which you can wear for the rest of your life), white button-down shirts, some sort of dark long pants that are mostly all the same color and not jeans, and black shoes. You can relax this dress code about three-quarters of the way through the book, but for now you still need to make the team.

For girls—girls already know what to wear, who am I kidding?

Another secret benefit of temping is that it actually saves you money on work clothes because you're always going to a different company every day. They have no idea you've been wearing the same tie/suit/dress for three years in a row. Only your haberdasher knows.

And one last thing before we embark on the odyssey of a lifetime:

Stress

Chill out. It's going to be hairy out there. Some days you're going to walk into hail storms. Other days you'll walk in and hear the sweetest sounds to a temp's ears: "It'll be slow today. I hope you brought a book." And I'll say, "I hope it's this one."

On hell days, which we'll go into in more detail in the "Survival Techniques" chapter, the main trick is: As long as you're prepared in advance, you'll walk out the other side unscathed. Keep this list inside you:

Chilling-Out Rules

◆ Don't worry about it.
◆ It's not your job.
◆ Go for a walk.
◆ Get out of the room for five minutes.
◆ Don't sweat it.
◆ Go to the bathroom.
◆ You'll never be back at this place again.
◆ You're just a temp.
◆ You don't care.
◆ These people are stupid.
◆ Very soon you'll be out of here and this won't ever have happened.
◆ You never have to come back here again.
◆ You're just a temp.
◆ Somebody who really cares about this job and is bucking for a promotion can sweat over it, but you're leaving at 5:00.
◆ Switch on autopilot, start typing, and resume daydreaming.
◆ Do only one thing at a time.
◆ Pretend you're a postal union worker.
◆ You're just a temp.
◆ Look at all the poor saps around you and realize they have to come back here every single day for the rest of their lives, but you'll never see this place again!
◆ Call your agency and end your assignment, and/or call a friend and have someone to talk to.
◆ Imagine the extremely large cocktail you're going to have very, very soon.
◆ It's not your job.
◆ You'll never be back.
◆ You're just a temp.

Stress is part of life. But not a temp's life! There's no reason to ever have stress again!

Let's Review

Get your typing speed up; pick one computer program and master it, then begin learning others; buy lots of cool stuff like telephones, Rollerblades, and beepers, but don't mistake *owning* something with *being* something; ride your bike to work whenever possible; there are more jobs out there than you could ever fill in a day, so if you don't like where you've landed, just spin the wheel one more time, because every time that wheel goes around, you're bound to cover just a little more ground.

4

-Your First Agent-

The whole deal is, counselors act as matchmakers by connecting one of the people who's available with one of the companies that's looking. That's the whole business right there.

Successful counselors have a knack for putting the right temp with the right company—a sort of human-connection instinct for who'll work well with whom.

What you as a temp need to find is a counselor who believes in you, understands you, and can place you in the right situations. If you don't find that connection, keep moving until you do. A positive, open working relationship with your counselor is one of the major keys to the game.

This may take the form of one particular agency where one counselor fulfills all your needs, but it may also take an entire office to satisfy the supercalifragilistic you. Just as every office has its own individual way of doing business, so too does each agency. Some are all business, some more creative; some are concerned with punctuality, others with how the tasks were performed; some like to establish a stable of temps and develop their skills, others prefer temps to know one trick and turn it forever. There are so many agencies out there, and you can apply at two or three a day, so it's only a matter of time before you make the magic connection.

Today's mission is to find that special person or agency that will get you the work you want to do. Here's how:

Try lots of agencies. This is not an exclusive arrangement. One agency won't mind if you temp through others because they know you're being trusted by someone else, and keeping your chops up, as they say on the bandstand. Even if you apply somewhere that only sends you out on one job or never sends you out at all, it's okay. This happens every day. Working is like fishing: you can't catch anything unless you cast your line.

True Story Department

I applied at this little off-the-wall agency that I only got one day's work out of, but on that one day I met someone who ended up hiring me for the next two years. Two years' work from a one-job agency! That's one of the thrills of temping—you never know when you leave your house each day how your life may change forever.

Connecting With Your Counselor

What you're ultimately trying to do in your agency search is to connect with one person. It's like dating. You'll take anything you can get, but what you're really looking for is that one-on-one connection with that extra magic *zing* where you're both floating on the same wavelength and the universe is flowing. This special she or he will become your key contact person and lifeline to the agency, the world, and the cash machine.

I'll use "counselor" and "agent" interchangeably since they're the same thing. This is the person at the agency (more often a she than a he) who will be calling you at home to offer you work and whose name you'll be asking for when you call in. This is the person you ultimately want to have a sixth-sense awareness with so that she is thinking of you and you are thinking of her at the exact same time a job is coming in.

She will be your guidance counselor when you're in trouble, and your booking agent for getting you work. She's your lifeline to employment and you should treat her with the courtesy you would a valued friend. Even though you sometimes get frustrated on the job, you wouldn't want to be mean to your friend because of it. Especially if she's going to be getting you work tomorrow.

If your agent doesn't behave toward you as a friend would—and sends you to places she *knowingly* misrepresents, or doesn't stick up for you, or doesn't have your best interests in mind—the sooner you stop associating with her, the stronger you'll be. And it's how you feel about yourself that determines how others feel about you.

If someone thinks so lowly of you they'd deceive you for their own benefit—whether it's your counselor, employer, buddy, or lover—it's not even a matter of self-esteem but of *self-preservation* that you immediately sever the relationship or you'll die of the poison. This is not a discretionary call. You will be killed if you allow it to spread. You're doing the other person as much harm as you are yourself by allowing dishonorable behavior to continue. Silence is complicity. Acquiescence allows the pattern to perpetuate. And teaching is the most honorable of professions.

Evaluating Agencies

When evaluating the agencies remember that both clients and temps tend to gravitate toward places where they feel most comfortable. Familiarity is where you'll feel at home and be surrounded by people more complementary to your plumage. Make a list of all the agencies that appeal to you, including their phone numbers, locations, and the benefits advertised. Here's how:

First

Pretend you need a temp. Open the Yellow Pages and look under "Employment—Temporary" for the ad that most grabs your eye. Some are conservative, some are funny; some stress databases and accounting, others stress graphics; some handle mostly day jobs, others stay open twenty-four hours; some offer $50 signing bonuses just for joining, and most offer similar referral bonuses for recommending other temps to their agency. Once your recom-

mended employee works a certain number of hours, usually forty or fifty, you receive a $50 or $100 bonus check. Most agencies are also now offering some affiliation with a health care provider. (See the "Health Care" section at the end for details.)

Second

Open the Help Wanted pages of your largest local newspaper and use similar personal criteria for scanning the ads geared toward temps, once again making a list of all the ones that look appealing to you, and write down the promises they make in the ad. If those promises don't hold up through your first interview, draw a line through their name, write a note as to why, and leave them on the list so you don't forget their name and fall for a new fake ad next year.

Third

Pick up the alternative and specialty publications in your area. These include neighborhood monthlies, arts listings, religious, and business publications. Many businesses like to target specific audiences with their employment searches. Write down a third list of which agencies you found in which specialty publications.

Fourth

Something many people don't try (but you should, and then you won't have to finish reading this book) is simply calling companies where you want to work. Businesses are more and more willing to hire employees for two or three days a week, for regular half-days, or on a freelance basis. By hiring you directly they'll not only gain a reliable, steady temp who's interested in the company but will avoid paying high agency fees for referring you. Call up the companies of your choice and tell them you're perfect for the job but can only work X hours. Employment is no longer thought of as permanent employees doing the 9 to 5. Even that phrase "9

52

to 5" is archaic. We're in the future here.

Okay, now you've got your three lists, and unless you plan to leave town soon, these should last you a while.

Fifth

Compare them. Mix and match. Look for agencies that showed up on more than one list; those are your key agencies. The magic connecting counselor to your future life as a freelance sailor surfing the network of cushy jobs is currently sitting at a desk in an office you have circled.

And speaking of global surfing, let's talk about the national temp agencies first. The biggest national temp agencies are: Kelly, Interim, Manpower, Olsten, Tiger, and Winston. One advantage to the big nationals is that they're the agencies who most frequently offer basic benefits like health coverage, a sign-up bonus, referrals, and even paid vacation days. But the other is the ability to change cities if you choose.

If you're not certain that your current city holds much of a future for you, registering at a large national agency with employment offices all over the country will open up the road to you. Most national agencies will transfer your employment records between cities. It's not like being a full-time employee at a major corporation with regional offices—there doesn't need to be an opening to transfer. As long as you have the skills, which you should have by the time you've read this book, just ask your counselor how the clams are cookin' in Frisco, and then wink.

I mean, I don't want to tempt you (ha-ha), and don't tell your mother where you heard this, but you can actually temp your way around the country on a permanent vacation, connecting each of the great cities with temp jobs so that you're never more than a half-day's drive to the next gig. I know it sounds crazy at first, but the more you drink beer and think about it, the more you'll want to drink beer and think about it.

On the Road

Focusing on only the nation's twelve largest temp cities in volume of business, begin naturally at the birthplace, Boston, Massachusetts, where the Mayflower rocks, man, and there's shots heard 'round the barstools 'round the clock, and tons of fat corporations all over the place paying fat suit-wearing dineros, plus there's a few cool schools to stock the pool with dating fools → to New York City, which, how can I put this? I've been sprinting at breakneck speed for fifteen years and can't get half of it done. But if at any point you want to continue your Great American Adventure cycling 'round the circle you can continue south to Philadelphia, the old Independence Hall bell ringing at sunrise routine when you're the only one there, soaking up the chimes of freedom ringing, before you split to the Nation's Capital where there's more free stuff to do than you can ever afford. You can temp your way from Oxon Run to Chevy Chase, but before you can say Smithsonian Institution in sixteen languages you boogie out of Bill town on your way to the Olympic Ghost Villages of Hotlanta, with the nicest bunch of cityfolk in Dixie and more corporate temping towers than the rest of the South combined → to New Orleans, which despite having the Funnest Quarter you'll ever flip, also has a booming temp industry and frozen margaritas sold like Slurpees in twenty-four different flavors twenty-four hours a day making it a little difficult to move, although your singing may improve. After several years of marinating in the madness, you may want to continue your circumference to the bright shiny towers of Houston to ride them fancy new eli-vators in one of the highest per-capita temp towns in the country, or drive on up the road to Dallas to sing the blues in Deep Ellum before making the longest trek of the trip to the goldmine of the desert, Phoenix, Arizona, the beginning of the movie *Psycho*. You can still rent a house in Tempe for $100 a month, and there's more canyons to hike than Manhattan, but once May rolls around and your car melts into a puddle and evaporates, you'll be catching the last train for the coast the day your music fried. You can stop in San Diego if you're searching for sailor boys in crewcuts with health plans, or L.A. if you want salvatious girls in low-cuts with dark tans, but after you've surfed the Waves of Dude and had the top of your head burnt like an egg on drugs, you may want to drive up the coast to San Francisco, which is Spanish for "Second Greatest City." There's a huge temping industry there, with the added bonus of harbors filled with beauty and streets full of happy. I can't imagine ever leaving but if you'd like to stick your head in the crown jewels of the West, continue up that cove-curving coast to the redwood spires of the Olympic peninsula located not far from the temping hotbed of Seattle. It's not a bad town if you like to do things like live a long time, bike, hike, or volleyball spike, plus it's an easy zoom up to Canada for a weekend to enjoy Vancouver, the city that's so surreally futuristic and gorgeous you think it's Disneyland's version of Cityland, the ultimate urban fantasy that somehow also seems to be a real live city with red cedar skyscrapers, hovercraft taxis, and Tinkerbell fairies flickering over fields of flowers beside water with mountains in it.

Like I say, it's a real hairbrained idea, but I'd do it again.

If surfing the country is an idea you're not sure whose time has come, here's a way to check it out without leaving town:

Temping on the Internet

If you type the word "temp agencies" in the search option of your Web browser, you'll get literally thousands of Web sites ranging from personalized reviews of certain cities to private agencies advertising their benefits to government employment agencies posting their job listings.

As you can imagine, the areas of specialization are endless. Here are a few addresses and/or site names reflecting the panoramic possibilities:

America's Employers; America's Help Wanted; America's Job Bank; Atlanta CyberJobs; Bay Area Job Location Finder; Boston Job Bank; California Career and Employment Center; Career Magazine (which includes on-line help for people 65 and over at http://www.careermag.com); Infosoft Group (created by the Wisconsin

Employment Bureau at http://www.isgrp.com/web); International Medical Placement; JobCenter (a national organization where anyone can post a resumé for $20 for six months, or a listing for a job for $5 a week), and everything is subject to automatic matching, USENET news feed distribution and regular job searches by anyone (http://www.jobcenter.com/); JobSAT, Canada's largest employment database covering all regions and professions (http://www.hookup.net/~jobsat/js-home.htm); Montana Job Service; National Employment Search; NationJob Network; Temp Access, a national organization connecting agencies with temps and temps with agencies (http://www.tempaccess.com/); and so on forever.

F.Y.I.: One of those "http://www" things is called a URL, which stands for Universal Resource Locator. Think of it as the "1" before a long distance phone number.

The National Association of Temporary Services has a web site that lists all affiliated agencies in all the major cities in North America (http://www.natss.com/staffing/)! Click on their Members/Database icon and you can look up, download, or print out a list of about fifty agencies in the next town you want to work in, including their phone numbers.

One of the advantages to job-searching on the net is that you can do it at home at night while maintaining your full-time job, or as a secondary supplement to daytime pavement pounding. Also, it's instantaneous: you can leave your resumé on fifty desks in one night, without leaving your room. You don't have to wait for the mail people to delay your delivery or have the recipient dread opening the stack with your paperwork. With e-mail responses you flash up as light on the monitors of their desks, and with electronic resumé posting you're allowing employers to find you via computer searches instead of you finding them. And perhaps best of all, until such time as every home is on-line, fewer people will be responding to the on-line postings than to the Help Wanted ads in local papers.

The principal drawback to on-line job-surfing is that by volume, more local jobs in your particular town are offered in that same Help Wanted section than you could find in a month of surfing the Net. Surf the Net to zero in, but read the paper to cover your turf.

The wondrous thing about the Internet is that no one knows where it's going to expand next or how. As long as small businesses continue to join large corporations in putting up Web sites and using e-mail and more temps continue to sign-on at home, more and more of the temping industry will be conducted via modem from here on out.

Picking the Agency for You

If you're one of those people who wants to go where everybody knows your name, and they're always glad you came, you may want to consider the local one-of-a-kind "Mom 'n' Pop" agencies. They're often more in tune with the nuances of your local community, plus they specialize; you can search for one that deals in the professional field(s) you're interested in and you'll be assured assignments in places you want to work.

Ask who an agency's clients are. If you're an actor, you should register at agencies that get a lot of work in advertising, networks, and special events. Agencies are becoming more and more specialized. Call your contacts, do some snooping—call every agency in the Yellow Pages if you have to—but find out who supplies the temps to the places you most want to work.

If, on your preliminary round of phone calls, they just tell you to come in to register, tell them you have a few questions and ask who you can speak with. You hold the power, they hold none. Remember that or we'll never get anywhere. You could work at a hundred agencies. You don't need them, but they can't keep their lights on without you doing their work for them, and doan you ever forget it.

A good way to start the phone call would be:

"I'm an excellent word processor [or whatever you are] and have a few questions. Who should I talk to?"

◆ Do not ask the receptionist of a temp agency questions

because she's just a call-forwarding director who answers a new line every 1.3 seconds.

◆ Even if you're not "excellent," since you're just looking for the truth, go ahead and lie.

Depending on how stressed the person you reach is at the moment, you should be able to get answers to many of the following questions:

◆ "Do you offer health insurance?"
◆ "A sign-up bonus?"
◆ "A 401k plan?"
◆ "How much work do you get in my field?"
◆ "Do you offer both temporary and permanent placement?"
◆ "Do you get work for all three shifts?"

These kinds of questions will help cross off some of the bad agencies from your list and narrow down your travel time. If you *don't* get a nice, helpful person on the phone, ask if there's a more convenient time you can call back. Sometimes temp agencies are fairly swamped with phone calls and job orders so they just can't talk at the moment. If they insist you come in and apply without answering any of your questions, cross that agency off your list and keep a note to never go in there. They don't have to tell you everything, but they should be able to give you a few answers, especially if you offer to call back at the more convenient time. If they aren't nice to you when they're trying to lure you in, they're going to be evil monsters when you work for them.

Let's Review

Find a straightforward, honest agent; if people disrespect you, shoot a hole in their phone number; apply to lots of agencies, but call first; go bumming around the country surfing the temp agencies and staying in all sorts of cool cities because you may as well try all the rides at the amusement park before you have to leave.

5

-Your First Interview-

For your first interview in person, I recommend applying at an agency that's *not* one of your top circled picks so you can work out the kinks on an out-of-town run-through before opening on Broadway. If you happen to score big and meet your magic counselor immediately, then you got lucky and are on your way. But since this usually doesn't happen, by trying your routine out somewhere inconsequential first, you'll know what to expect and give a much better performance in all subsequent interviews.

Sometimes you must schedule an appointment, so call first. For the agencies that prefer walk-ins, ask the time range when new applicants can come in, then pick the time of day within their window that you're at your sharpest. If you're still working a regular shift and have trouble getting time off to interview, explain this to the agencies on your initial call. Good agencies will offer to set up a 5:30 interview if that's the only time you can come in. Remember, they're looking for workers even more than you're looking for work.

At many agencies where I've worked for years, the only time I ever physically walked in their door was the day of the interview. My counselor and I never laid eyes on each other again but did thousands of dollars worth of business together for years. Point:

there's only about one hour of this whole entire process that you actually have to be bright-eyed and awake, and the interview is it.

When you go in they'll ask you for a resumé with references, and federal law requires providing your proof of citizenship. Bring two forms of ID, one with photo, to every interview (passport and driver's license are good; library card is not). You'll have to take a typing test, maybe a spelling and grammar test, sometimes a math test (bring in your own pocket calculator, it's okay), and finally a test on the computer programs you claim to know. You can see why it's advantageous to first run through this embarrassing ritual at a place where nobody you know will see you.

Acing the Tests

Be accurate and be careful. Don't be so slow as to seem stupid, but timing won't fail you, whereas mistakes will. What you score on their tests is the only physical record the agency will ever have of your abilities, so it's important to score high.

For the typing test, the agency will let you warm up on the typewriter or computer they're testing you on. Take advantage of this time. Use the watch I suggested you buy in chapter 3 to time a full five-minute test on yourself so when the timed test comes you know how far you have to type to beat your practice score. Memorize the practice test as best you can because often they won't change it for the test, so you can run through it in your mind and be aware of where the tricky bits are.

Most agencies now use a standardized typing test computer program with one glitch you need to know about: it will allow you to correct only the word you're currently in on the document, so if you look up at the screen and spot an error in the previous sentence—or even two words back—don't try to fix it. If you try to go back, an error beep will sound and your screen will freeze for a valuable second of typing time.

The computer software testing programs are another reason to apply first at an agency you don't really care about because you'll get to preview the computerized tests they use for the specific program(s) you use. There are only a few of these computer testing programs on the market, and I've been asked exactly the same questions at several different agencies.

A computer prompt will instruct you to perform a series of tasks, such as: "Change the margins of this document to one and a half inches on the left and right." And then you have to hit the exact keystrokes to do so. You're permitted only two attempts per task, so hit the right keys.

Always bring a template if you're used to using one. You can't depend on the agency to have one for your program because they test people on fifty different programs. Templates are allowed because you're expected to be able to look at one on the job, but not everybody knows to bring one, so this is another slight advantage to you.

Before going in, run through the exact strokes of most functions of the programs you're applying for because you may have some little keystroke quirk you use that would give you a technically wrong answer even if it ultimately performed the task. The computer testing program is looking for the most direct, fewest-keystroke method for performing the requested task.

As you can see there are a lot of steps in this dance routine, and your out-of-town rehearsal can mean the difference between a long run and a short season.

Your Counselor and You

Your counselor/agent is the key to your success. Here are just a few of the things you'll be talking to her about in the next year or two:

- ◆ You're sick and can't make it to a job
- ◆ You're on a job and get sick
- ◆ You're having car trouble, train trouble, or alarm trouble and are going to be late
- ◆ Your assignment has been extended
- ◆ Your assignment has been terminated

◆ Your skills have improved (you've learned a new program, etc.)

◆ Your responsibilities on an assignment have increased (you went in on a job as a receptionist and ended up replacing a legal secretary)

◆ The client approaches you about working without the agency

◆ You're injured on the job

◆ You've accepted a long-term job through another agency or on your own

◆ You'll be appearing in a play for the next two months and won't be available.

Even if you disappear for a long time, bimonthly check-ins are a nice touch. If you keep the call short (or follow her lead if she starts to chat), calling in is a professional courtesy and accepted behavior.

Your counselor will always help deflect or absorb client criticism, but you have to let her in on your status as soon as you know it. Remember, she's on your team and this is the relationship you need to maintain in order to be a successful temp.

If after a while your counselor should leave the agency and go to another one, which happens, and you're on good terms with her, you'll hopefully know about it in advance and can transfer with her. You're not supposed to do this because she's not supposed to take her favorite temps with her when she changes agencies, but it happens all the time. You have to pretend you just coincidentally went into that new agency and applied. It's accepted and under- stood that this occurs, but it's professional to do it quietly.

You don't have to switch agencies, but if you can, it's better than destroying the valuable alliance and personal relationship you've cultivated over hundreds of hours of phone time and months or years of working together. Of course you can also retain your relationship with the first agency and simply continue working with their other counselors. So instead of losing a counselor you've gained a new agency.

As I'll remind you constantly, this is a business of relationships. It's the rapport between agent and temp that creates much of the work in this industry. Your agent must know you and your skills and match them most effectively with a company in need. That matchmaking skill is part of what keeps this business growing year after year.

The Interview

This may be the only time your counselor ever lays eyes on you, so a good first impression is crucial. Be relaxed. Be yourself, because yourself is the best thing you've got. If you're nervous and sweaty and shaking and stupid, then that's what they'll remember, as in, "Oh, let's call that nervous, sweaty, shaking stupid person."

But if you're kind of funny and loose and goofing and seem like you've been there a million times, then they'll love you. Although sometimes actually they hate that. Sometimes you want to be totally straight, get a haircut, be really normal. Play it however you sense it should be played—only don't sweat. They hate that.

Again, what you're looking for is a relationship. You want to feel comfortable with the person you interview with because it's she who will give the rest of the agency the review of you. Agencies rely on the instincts and conclusions of the person who interviews you. *Make eye contact.* If you feel like you can connect and be honest with this person, then pursue it. Look around at the other people in the office. Take special note of them. They're taking note of you.

The in-person interview is the part where you have to bond with the office. They're going to be your source of food for the indefinite future. Do you like 'em or not? As you eavesdrop on conversations in the busy office, consider: Are these the type of people you want to be dealing with? Are these people like you, or are they dangerous aliens? This is the moment to decide: Are you one of them?

There are no tips: I won't b.s. you and say sit up straight. The truth is, counselors at agencies know people as well as anyone on earth. That's why they get into the business—they love people. And every single day they evaluate about a hundred new ones. It's their job to monitor and rate these new applicants and then measure how they pan out in the field. Around the office, each counselor tries to have a better record than anyone else at picking the good apple—temps and discarding the bad. So these people are masters, like curators at a top museum, and they can spot a fake before it's half unwrapped.

If you even remotely try to pull anything over on them they'll know it so fast they'll have you out the door in their mind before you've even finished the sentence. If there are holes in your resumé because you were a junkie or in jail or a Republican or anything else you're ashamed of, it's better you tell them because then they'll know you're honest and that's the whole entire key.

This is a business of trust. Sometimes temps feel it's not important whether they even show up for the job they've been assigned to. This happens all the time even though so much is riding on it. First and foremost is the relationship between the agency and the client. Scores of other temps are relying on that relationship to stay solid. If you don't show, you're letting down your brethren of temps who built the net you surf in.

And with that in mind, be straight-up with your counselor, look 'em in the eye, and show 'em respect. Have the time-hole blanks in your resumé filled with well-rehearsed reasons or the truth, and be clear on why you're looking for work right now. They are right to be suspicious of people who walk in off the street and can't clearly explain why they lost their last job. If your excuse is you were sick of where you worked because you were being treated poorly for no good reason, that's a legitimate reason for changing jobs.

Be honest with yourself before you go in, and practice a one-sentence answer to the question: "Why did you leave this job?"

You'll also be asked:

◆ What rate do you want?
◆ What computer programs do you know?

◆ What kinds of companies are you interested in?
◆ What shifts can you work?
◆ Are you interested in short- or long-term?
◆ What have you been doing since your last job?
◆ Do you do word processing "Center" work?
◆ Who's your favorite Beatle?
◆ Are you interested in a permanent job?

Determining Your Rate

Determine your rate in advance. The agent will ask you what is the lowest rate you'll accept. Don't be fooled—the rate you quote as "the lowest you'll accept" will become your standard. The agency will never voluntarily offer you more than this lowest rate until you earn and demand a raise, take on more difficult programs, or work less desirable shifts. So ask high. The worst that can happen is you'll have to compromise down to the rate you were expecting anyway. But if you admit right off the bat you'd work for $X today, it'll be hard to convince your agent to give you $Y tomorrow.

Alternate Route

If they insist they send people out at a lower rate than you know is the going rate for good temps, tell the agent, "Okay, I'll work for you for two weeks at your rate, but if I get glowing reports, I expect you to up me to my rate." Agents will often agree to this because if they know you know the rate and are considering other agencies, they don't want to lose you. And the funny part is you've just guaranteed yourself a raise in your third week of work.

You Interview Them

While you're still there in the chair, be sure not to leave until you have the answers to all the following questions:
◆ Do they offer free computer courses or training time? When? Do you need an appointment?

- What's their guaranteed minimum payment for cancelled assignments?
- What's their bonus for referring other temps to the agency? How soon do you get it?
- What kind of health plan do they offer? After how many hours worked?
- Do they offer vacation pay? A 401k plan?
- What kinds of clients do they have in the field of _____? (your preferred profession here)
- Is there help finding permanent work?
- What's the payroll procedure for submitting timesheets and issuing checks? How long is the delay between work and paycheck?

It's okay to write down their answers in shorthand as you're talking.

Once you begin your life as a temp, you'll go out in the field and work and then come back and repeat the interviewing process at a new agency when you're ready to expand. Even an old hound dog like me still goes through this after all these years. You'll forever be courting new agencies, energy, people, and leads. So take notes. It will improve your grade for next time.

Long-term vs. Short-term

Long-term assignments can last anywhere from a week to a month to a year. The benefits are security, the chance for a permanent job, a regular check at a predetermined amount, and no worry about booking your next assignment. Long-term assignments are good for people who don't like constant change.

vs.

Short-term jobs last from a day to a week, and their benefits are freedom, flexibility, variety, adventure, less structure, opportunity to evaluate different companies, and choosing your own days off and vacation time without having to answer to anyone. Short-term jobs allow for spontaneity in your other pursuits because you don't have to commit your time more than a day in advance, and you'll never fall into a negative working rut for longer than a week.

Stand-by Policy

"Stand-by" policy means you can go into an agency between 7 and 9 A.M. "standing by" for the first assignment you're qualified for. Coming into an agency on stand-by is most commonly used by people who have an hour or more commute into the Central Business District where the bulk of the jobs are. Since most temp agencies locate themselves in the proximity of the offices they serve, being at the agency makes you only minutes from any given assignment.

The advantages are: you're sitting in front of the counselor ready to go instead of being another voice on a phone in a distant neighborhood; you're the first to be sent out—also because it doesn't look real good if there's a bunch of temps crowding the waiting room with no work as the new applicants begin showing up to interview; you earn an extra hour's pay because you're at the job sooner; you earn brownie points with your counselor because standing by shows you're serious and eager to be working; you can utilize downtime while you're there to learn a new program on their computers; plus, it makes the agency look good because they're promptly filling a job—with you!

The disadvantage is there may be no work and you came in for nothing. Ask what your agency's policy is. If there's no work, most agencies will pay you a guaranteed minimum—usually two hours—for coming in and waiting around on what should properly be called "sit-by." So bring a book (maybe this one!) and let words turn the hours to minutes.

Clients Testing Temps

One of the biggest changes in temping in the last few years has been an increase in client's requests to screen temps before employing them. Generally a company that calls a temp agency to ask for a temp is supposed to trust the agency's screening process to provide a competent temporary employee. However, some large clients or clients who deal in sensitive areas want to be more involved in the screening process and are requesting that temps come in for a personal interview and/or testing session at the company before being allowed to work there. In some cases you're paid for this time, but in most cases you're not.

It's your decision whether to go for these interviews. Since this is usually done for long-term assignments, you may consider your time investment worth it. If you prefer short-term jobs, this won't come up too often, but it has emerged as a fact of life in Templand.

If it happens, bring your resumé and be prepared to go through a one-to-three hour screening process. They'll often ask for multiple temps to come in for only one job opening. Not fun. If you want to specialize in legal, brokerage, or other high-paying, high-sensitivity fields, be prepared for the possibility of in-house testing, and have your mind made up in advance whether you want to go in and win the job this way—or wait for a more comfortable gig that doesn't make you bob for apples.

Timesheets

Before you leave they'll give you a stack of timesheets which look sort of like credit card charge slips. These are for recording the hours you've worked at each assignment, and you must fill them out and get them signed by a supervisor before you leave each job site.

Each agency has its own policy of how to submit timesheets for payment but it's usually along the lines of phone, fax, and/or mail your timesheets in by Friday or Monday, and your paycheck's ready on the Tuesday or Wednesday following the week you worked.

Ask. When you're in at the agency be sure you get their exact payroll procedure, and if they try to hold back your check longer than the week following when you worked, then there's something wrong and you shouldn't work for that agency. There are too many good ones out there, and they're all looking for skilled temps. If an agency is in any way uncooperative in issuing your check, they don't deserve your services, and they may be close to insolvent.

Because timesheet fraud became a big problem during the temp boom of the 1980s, many safeguards have now been designed into agency payroll procedures. Some agencies require seeing signed timesheets and confirming the hours with the client before they'll even fill out a check request. This sometimes causes delays in payment, and in the case of some agencies, is so cumbersome that checks are delayed by weeks. You won't work for these agencies very long.

Paychecks

Paychecks are one of the "catches" in the temping business. Since you won't be receiving an identical paycheck each week as you would at a permanent job, you have to scrutinize every paycheck carefully to make sure the hours, rate, and overtime have all been calculated correctly. Some temp agencies will try to cheat you. They'll pay you a lower rate than your counselor quoted you, deduct hours, not pay you the hourly rate breakdown you worked, and so on. Whether this is due to incompetence or slippery ethics is open to speculation, but the fact is check cheating happens a lot.

It's your responsibility as the temp to check your pay stubs carefully. Even after fifteen years of doing this and working with the most ethical agencies, I still check every single pay stub (which is attached to your check), and still find mistakes every single year.

If you find an error, no matter how small, immediately contact the payroll office at your agency and point out the inconsistency. If you catch a mistake the first time, even if it only amounts to a $6 adjustment, and badger them about it until they cut you a new check, they're less likely to screw up next time.

Sealing the Deal and Following Up

After you've aced the tests, bonded with the counselor, and the interview is over, ask, "Do you have anything right now?" And they usually say, "No," because they don't know you yet. Then you say, "Okay, well, I should be available next week. I'll be out applying at some other agencies for the rest of this week." At which point they say, "Wait, I might have something," and you may have your first assignment before you leave the office.

Once you leave the interview and preferably before you do anything else, take anywhere from five minutes to an hour to write notes about all the names you can remember and who they were and what they looked like; the details of what they said; your immediate impressions of the office; your initial gut feeling about the counselor and the agency; and what you think you said or did wrong that you can correct before your next interview.

I recommend a different pad of paper for each agency because you may end up writing several pages of notes on the interview, plus jotting down details on subsequent phone calls regarding jobs and so on. This way you've got a separate palette to work from for each agency.

You may be going to many different agencies in a short period of time and you must be able to distinguish them. Through the process of establishing yourself in the temp world you're going to meet many new people. Calling someone by their wrong name is a great way to diminish a resource.

Let's Review

Temping is a good thing; be honest and look people in the eye; do well on the tests because that's the only written record they have of you; take careful notes, learn from everyone, and don't take *@&! from anyone.

6

-Your First Booking-

After the insanely long process of testing and interviewing comes the slightly trickier step of actually getting your first job. This may seem impossible right now as you're reading this book, but you have nothing to worry about with me in your sidebag. We'll be on the job in no time.

Timing

Ask your counselor the best time to call in the morning. Call at exactly that time. Then begin experimenting—if you call five minutes sooner do you get the answering service, or does the early bird counselor get you working before the other worms have crawled up?

After you call in and are having your toast and eating it too, it's a good time to grab your agency notepads and record the exact time you called each agency, whom you spoke to, what she or he said, the vibe, and your impressions.

What you're trying to do is cast your line in the River of Employment just as the hammerhead jobfish is swimming by. Some people call in their availability at 8 A.M. and then sit back and wait for the phone to ring. Others call every fifteen minutes until they've become so annoying the agency has them arrested. Both are mistakes.

Record each call on that agency's specific notepad. Monitor the results and modify your call-time. You need to rely a little bit on intuition, a little bit on logic, and a little bit on reading the tone of the voice of the person who answers the phone when you call.

During quieter times of the day, you may want to ask your counselor when the offices you want to work for call in their job orders. This varies; advertising, catering, and graphics companies usually call later in the morning than law firms and banks. Exact times vary from city to city, profession to profession, company to company. It's the kind of information that's unique to each situation and why you want to have a clear, communicative relationship with your counselor.

Hot Time, Spring Is in the City

If you call an agency several times after what you thought was a successful interview and you get no jobs, remember some seeds never bloom, while others lay dormant before springing up like Jack's beanstalk. If things are slow, go sow another agency. Whole worlds emerge when a new agency begins sending you to all-new places. You can harvest an August bounty every time you rattle off a few more tests somewhere.

I'm not just using these metaphors purely for the fun of it. An employment agency really is a garden where anything can sprout at any time. Seeds are planted that might not grow for years. A good impression here, a specific interest there, and a job and an applicant from two different walks of life can be connected in a way that changes both of their lives. This happens every day at every good temp agency in the world. You want to tend this garden well. Is it the kind of soil your seed can take root in? Or does it feel arid, foreign, and unfriendly? While you're in their office, hold your dandelion high and blow its fluff puffs across the field, because it may not be the first counselor you talk to, but someone else who overhears your voice or reads your resumé, and who knows just the conditions for you to flower.

Tend your garden. If business is slow, you may have done well and they want to give you work, but there's a lull for whatever seasonal reason. Be calm and be cool. If you got a good vibe off them and they seem genuinely enthusiastic about you, keep checking in even if it drops off to once every week or two. By performing a continual random survey of their business flow you keep in the counselor's mind and appear consistent. A steady, patient hand often brings dormant seeds to bloom.

Talking Your Way in the Door

Sometimes if it's really busy, agencies will have receptionists write down everyone's availability. This is okay and can get you work, but calling back a half hour or more later and speaking to your own counselor is worth the second effort. You can see why I recommend the notepads and careful notation of call times. In pencil, after you've written down the time of the call, skip a line and write down the next time to call back. This way, if you look at your agency's notepad, the bottom line will immediately tell you the time of your next call.

Always be nice to the receptionist. If you're nasty, mean, short-tempered, or condescending, the receptionist will ask who the creep with your name is when she and your counselor are making small talk in the quiet hours of the afternoon. If the counselor hears that you're less than professional with the agency's own staff, she'll rightfully worry that you may offend a client or a client's customer.

Be nice. It's profitable.

Don't be off-put if you call in the morning and get put off. Try it for a few days and if you don't get work in a week, speak to your agent to find out what's going on. This procedure of writing down your availability is some agencies' very efficient way of managing the morning rush, and other agencies' way of avoiding you. Monitor and modify your approach according to the work you're getting. Confirm the agency's phone-in policy with your counselor. Follow orders—at least in the beginning, if only to prove to your agent that you can—then modify to get results.

During the 8–9 A.M. morning rush, phone calls should always be quick, to the point, and over in less than a minute, while still being polite, poignant, funny, and articulate. Okay, I'll give you an example, but then you have to do it yourself.

OTHER VOICE: "Hello, Your New Agency."

YOU: "Hi, is Sandy there?"

OV: "Sorry, she's not in yet."

YOU: "Is Enid there?" (Drawing on random name you overheard while interviewing with Sandy.)

OV: "Just a minute."

ENID: "This is Enid."

YOU: "Enid, this is [your name here]. I aced some [your program here] tests with Sandy yesterday and she told me to call in first thing this morning and I'm ready to go." (Say this all cheery and energetic and coffee-buzzed, with the emphasis on "rrr-eady to go," like Tony the Frosted Flakes Tiger so you're conveying the information but sounding playful in the blizzard of her stress.)

E: "Oh, great. What's your name?"

YOU: "[see above]"

E: "Do you do Windows?"

YOU: "Yes." ("But they're extra.") (No, don't say that.)

E: "Hold on."

YOU: (Hear music for a few seconds.)

E: "Have you ever worked at Greed & Avarice before?"

YOU: "No." (Hint: be truthful.)

E: "Okay, look—I'm going to take a chance and send you there. This place is very corporate. Can you handle that?" (Meaning look like a robot and act like one, too.)

YOU: "Yeah." (If you can't walk into the middle of a corporate office without looking like some clown in an orange jumpsuit with an armful of balloons, then this line of work may not be for you.)

The Conformity Clause

No matter how orange you may be on the inside, you have to be able to make yourself gray on the outside for a short stretch of time or you can't swing in the money tree. Remember, as a temp you're an undercover spy. None of us is a part of the worlds we infiltrate. None of us fits. That's why we're here. And it's more than okay. Seeing the railroad ties who do this for life just reinforces why we don't. It's a good idea to put the clown suit in the bag for a few hours so you can soak up some new material in Straightsville.

> E: "They're at the intersection of X and Y. How soon can you be there?"
>
> YOU: (The correct answer is one hour or less from now.)
>
> E: "Okay, good. You report to Linda Lennon on the eighth floor. Her phone number extension is 1206."

Always get first and last names and the phone number because if you show up somewhere and it's the reception desk of a huge company with two thousand employees and you just say, "Linda," you'll waste valuable time trying to find that person and you'll appear late for the assignment. Sometimes in the urgent rush of the morning the agent forgets to give you all the information. It's up to you to ask. If you get somewhere and don't know where you're going, it's not the agent who'll look dumb. It's up to you to secure:

◆ Both names of the person you're reporting to and their title and extension
◆ The exact location, including floor and office
◆ An estimated time of arrival

In the morning rush, you may not always get all of it, but that's the goal.

Advance booking questions: If this is not a rushed morning assignment but rather a booking made in the afternoon for tomorrow, you can ask:

◆ What kind of place is it?
◆ What do they do?
◆ How long have they been in business?
◆ Is it a busy place?
◆ How long has the agency worked with them?
◆ Do other temps want to go back?

Gather as much information as you can. "Knowledge is power," as old Francis Bacon said. But General Robert E. Lee put it cooler: "The most powerful weapon in any army is intelligence."

E: "I'll tell Sandy that I sent you out. Don't let us down. This place is really tough, so be on your toes."

YOU: This is a really good time to say "I just want to confirm my rate on this." (If you ask now when they're desperate rather than tomorrow when you're history, you'll probably get the most favorable result. If they quote you low, a good thing to say is: "I'll do this now because you need me, but Sandy and I were talking more in the $X to $Y range for this sort of job." Then Enid might say, "Hold on, let me see what I can do," and put you on hold. The rates are pretty much locked in and there may only be a dollar or two leeway, but if there is any, you'll win it *before* going in to the assignment, not after.)

Do not haggle with them early in the morning when they're rushing to fill spots. Bail them out. Go do the job. Get it done, win the point and soon you should be getting more raises and jobs than you know what to do with. If you're one of those customers who's a pain in the ass to deal with, they may leave you standing there and serve someone else breakfast tomorrow.

To close the call and send you out the door, the Secret Agent says: "Thanks a lot. Knock 'em dead."

And your first mission begins! YEEEEAAAAAA!!!!!

We're going to our first temp job!

See how easy that was!

Boom! Now we're sailing!

I'll go with you this time as I promised, but then you have to do one yourself.

Let's Review

Always be a good person; carefully monitor the time of your calls to each agency and record the results; get all information on assignments before hanging up the phone; confirm your rate before taking the job; learn new things; enjoy your life.

7

-Your First Day-

Hi-ho, hi-ho, it's off to work we go. ♪ ♪ ♪

This is the funnest part—the unknown. Each day's wondrous adventure begins with only an address and whatever other information you could suss out of the SecretAgent. These little coded numbers are the glints of glitter we glimpse that lead us to the gold.

Temping is not like playing a lottery where it's designed for you to lose; with temping you win every time you play because something interesting always happens, and you come home a wiser, richer soul, and a tangibly wealthier person.

I live in New York City, in case you couldn't tell from my accent, and after fifteen years of adventuring on the jobstreets of Metropolis I've worked on virtually every block in town, strolled down every interesting street, ridden every high-speed elevator, snuck on every good-view rooftop, and I just keep temping. It's so keen! You're never in the same place twice—unless you want to be. And if you are, you've got a line on the inside track.

If you luck out and win a pleasant place to work in, you can continue returning to your golden goose (see Aesop for more details); if it's bad, you never have to go back again. Either way you'll be meeting new people, working in new places, and learning new stuff!

True Story Department

One of the worst jobs I ever had temping—I had to work the whole time if you can imagine—was at a maritime law firm. They dealt with ships and importing and how much it costs to hold cargo per hour and all this really interesting stuff I never thought about. For one day I was on the inside of the business reading the private contracts between foreign exporters and domestic importers about harbor captains and ships being held up in foreign ports and cargo being confiscated. On the walls they had detailed oceanographer maps of harbors from all around the world and it was all stuff I would never have known anything about except for my one day standing on the helm of that intriguing ship.

They made me type all day so of course I never went back, but it just goes to show you that even if you have to actually work it can still be fun.

The Out-the-Door Checklist

In your hand or handbag you want to keep handy:

◆ the address and phone number your counselor just gave you
◆ templates or cheat sheets for the program you're using
◆ timesheets from the agency
◆ backup material to keep you busy during downtime
◆ a blank diskette in case you create anything you need later
◆ a blank file folder to begin a file on the place you're going
◆ cash for supplies to avoid time wasted in bank lines

Arriving Prepared

First of all, if it's remotely possible to be five minutes early—do it. Personally I'm fifteen minutes late so regularly that my agencies tell me to be there fifteen minutes earlier than the client expects me so I'll walk in on time. But I wouldn't recommend this your first week.

The other reason you want to be early is because the coordinates provided by your SecretAgent may not be 100 percent accurate, and you may have to use your map and detective's nose to sniff out the hidden job.

Let's say in some sort of a wild fictional sense that you actually arrive on time. All the while, before you got there, you should be going over and over your contact's name in your head so it just rolls off your tongue. "Hello, Linda, nice to meet you." "Hello, Linda! Really nice to meet you." "Linda! What's happening!" Practice, practice, practice.

Remember: This is a business of relationships. The personnel supervisor at the company will be able to read you as well as the counselors at the agency. She'll know where you slept last night and what you had for breakfast before you've finished shaking hands. And this is your five minutes to win her over before she leaves you at your workstation for the day.

Why, you ask, am I going into all this detail about just one job? Perhaps it's time for →

The Philosophy of Temping

What you want to do here is milk the cash cows (there'll be more on this in "Milking the Cows"). As you work from place to place, you can choose the jobs you like and return to them again and again, or you can go from long-term assignment to long-term assignment and work in a new place only every few months. I'll cover all options in excruciating detail as we go—but at the beginning you want to Surf the Wave.

You're not looking for one job—you're looking for a series of clients that want you back and that you want to go back to. That's why I recommend keeping notes on each job you go to; even if it's a bad one, make a note that reminds you why. If the agency tries to send you back there next year you might mistakenly register it as an "Oh-Yeah-I've-Been-There" good-vibe association. Whereas if you've got a note that says, "Cheap bigots," you may decide to pass.

As quickly as possible during the day you want to make the personal decision of whether you're coming back or not. There are so many great places to work, there's no reason to return to a crummy one—unless you didn't make a note and forgot you were there before. As Mario Cuomo always used to say, "Fool me once, shame on you. Fool me twice, shame on me."

"If you ain't singing where you're standing, honey, you ain't in the choir." I said that.

The Legendary Ben McReynolds

If you like the looks of the jobsite, take note of the company as a place you want to come back to. This way, a week or year from now you can call your counselor and ask, "Hey, what about Greed & Avarice? I haven't been there for a while."

This may be followed by your SecretAgent saying, "Let me market you in there." By keeping your own list with dates and comments on the places you go, over time you create a bank account you can draw on. It's the old "Hey-What-About" routine, first used by the Legendary Ben McReynolds, the 1930s food wrap salesman from the South. He kept more records than a deejay and did more business than Dow Jones. The Legendary Ben never stayed anywhere too long, never set down roots we could trace, but laid out routes we could follow. He stayed where he liked, and moved when it moved him. Everyone knew him, and he always did what he was there to do.

As Ben frequently reminded us, "When I was seventeen I walked into the jungle, and when I was twenty-one, I walked out. And, by God, I was rich!" Be proud. Temping has a glorious and heroic heritage, and now *you* are about to become a part of it! The colorful, the charismatic, the brave! Earn all that you can earn.

Climb every staircase, forge every intersection. Do not go gentle into that good life. Pick your chicken and eat it, too. These are the rhymes that warm men's souls in the winter of our unemployment. And I mean every word surreally.

So there you are at your first day on the job, and you meet—what's her name?

Remember? Can you tell me? See, I intentionally distracted you with that Ben McReynolds story to see if you'd forget the name you were supposed to be repeating over and over in your head and now it's back on the previous page and you can't even cheat without flipping the page back and getting zapped by a bolt of karmalightning. I'm sorry, but if you can't remember you have to go all the way back to chapter 1 and start over.

The rest of us will continue on to our new desk, rapidly assimilating all information around us like Data on *Star Trek*, memorizing as much as we can about the hallways, terminals, strange stares or sweet smiles we collect along the way.

You want to make as good an impression on Mmm Mmmm as possible during this walk, because this is a business of _____. If she likes you, you've got lunch money for the next year. If she doesn't, you go hungry, bow-bow-bow.

Be cool. Personally I grab a pad of paper and start writing everything down without taking my eyes off her while listening as clearly as I can. These first moments are always the hardest. As anyone who's ever performed on a stage will tell you: till you reach your stride, fall into the pocket, and connect with the audience—you're in limbo hell.

Look Mmm Mmmm in the eye. Make contact. Listen to what she's saying. Write it down if you have to, including names—especially that of the closest secretary or coworker. That bond is the next step to making this work.

But psst! Beware: You get close to some people by making friendly conversation—and you get close to others by not speaking at all. A common mistake of overeager rookie puppies is to try and make everyone love them by being cute and entertaining. Remember what it was like when you had a full-time job and hated your life? The last thing you wanted was some perky temp chattering away like a radio you can't turn off.

Hopefully you made a good impression on Mmm Mmmm at least. That was your five minutes, babe, I hope you made the most of it. You just said goodbye to the main person at the jobsite who'll be hiring you or not hiring you.

The Desk's the Thing

Perform the following procedure, in approximately this order, upon first arrival at every new temp site:

1. Figure out the phones. Use Post-its to mark the correct names on each phone line; in fact, you can even write down exactly what you're supposed to say, like, "Mr. So-and-so's office," or the company name or whatever the exact words are so you won't draw a blank when you pick up the strange phone.

2. Log on to the computer first thing and make sure it's working. Explore the hard disk or network drives, familiarizing yourself with the directories. Send one page to the printer so you know it prints and where.

3. Who's the big boss? Get a quick overview so you don't hang up on the president. Who's your boss? Check in with him or her, whether that means a wave, a nod, a handshake or a conversation. If there's work to be done, do it first without hesitation. It wins you the biggest first impression points you can score, plus it gets you involved, focused, and in the game.

4. Find the in-box of stuff for you to do. Open the mail. Orient yourself to your desk. Make sure you have all of the supplies you need for basic operation within reach. Perform an entire desk setup early so you're prepared for any influx of work, or at least so you can do your own work later if you get the chance. Don't be scared—be prepared.

5. Make laser beam eye contact with everyone you meet. I'm

not talking a blinking flash. We're talking Obiwan Kenobi eye-lock melt down. Nail 'em. See right through to their soul—and then they won't bug you the rest of the day.

6. Look on the computer or in a file for a copy of a letter, memo, proposal or whatever you're working on, in his or her preferred format. This is a key to getting things right the first time with many bosses, at least those for whom "right" means "the way my secretary does it." You may have a better system, a better-looking format for a memo or letter, but keep it to yourself. It will look foreign, unfamiliar, and wrong. Always emulate the regular secretary's style. Bosses are used to seeing things a certain way and get very nervous if anything is new and different (even if it's better). They'll want you to re-do it the "right" way, the way Sally the Secretary always does it. So you may as well do it that way the first time.

7. Call your counselor with your direct phone number, and remind her of your availability for the rest of the week. Fill out your timesheet with everything but your ending time and put it somewhere you can see it so you'll remember to have it signed before you leave.

8. Learn everyone's name. Find the company's exact name, pronunciation, and address. Learn where you are within the office. Find the fax and photocopy machines and make sure you know how they work.

9. Look through the materials on the desk to familiarize yourself with the concepts of the company, and some of the names of people involved in your workstation. Explore around the hard disk and try to find the exact subdirectory the regular person was working in yesterday so you can scan the documents and be there waiting when revisions come around. You need to be ready to instantly leap into any massive document or whatever task you're there to do. It's the optimum state of readiness that you're striving to achieve in those first hours. Know the people, the ropes, the

bathroom, the floor plan, the computer's directory tree. Know yourself.

Now go get a cup of coffee, you've earned it.

The whole morning of the first day you're under the Eagle Eye Scrutiny Rules. If you pass muster they'll stop watching you by lunch and you can slowly begin to assume control of the company, but for the first morning you should appear busy.

First impressions are lasting. Therefore, do not talk on the phone. Even though people seem to ignore temps, don't make the mistake of thinking you're invisible. I've seen people obliviously talking on the phone by the hour so everybody in a twelve-foot radius could hear them. A lot of temps use the phone, but it's one of the easiest ways to get an immediate strike against you. Every personnel supervisor asks the secretary who sat near you how much of a talker you were. Not being a blabbermouth while you're trying to win over the company is one of the easiest ways you can win a gold typewriter ribbon toward Radar's Hall of Temporary Fame.

The Radar O'Reilly Temporary Hall of Fame

Named for the greatest administrative assistant the world has ever known, Corporal Walter Eugene "Radar" O'Reilly, who served in the M*A*S*H 4077th Unit from the movie in 1970 through his honorable discharge nine years later. First under Colonel Henry Blake, then Colonel Sherman Potter, Radar's clairvoyance in anticipating the needs of his vaguely bosslike commanding officers set the benchmark to which all of us aspire.

His Spockian ear-perked pronouncements—"Choppers"— seconds before regular humans could detect them, is still a code word used by temps to signal trouble on the way. With Gene Kelly grace he'd glide through the door and slip the report into the colonel's hand at the precise moment he realized he wanted it.

Radar has been an inspiration to us all. He's the Babe Ruth of clerical workers. If you ever get a Trivial Pursuit question about

Temps just answer "Radar O'Reilly" and you'll probably get the pie slice. He holds virtually every record. He was the only man to play himself in both the movie and TV show about his life. His combination of childlike innocence, practical midwestern ethics, and a supernatural ability to read others' minds made him a leader among men but gave him an unfair advantage at cards.

If you ever hear your counselor say, "Have a Radar day," what they're really saying is: Be unreal. Be beyond good. Be transcendent! Work thirty-three hour days, score hat tricks, seal the deal, save the day, fix a computer, troubleshoot a problem, solve the crime, make damn fine coffee, take a few notes here, win a few friends there, sniff out some secrets, and solve a few mysteries—*these* are what make an Honorary Radarian.

If you collect enough gold typewriter ribbons, you'll be eligible for the Radar O'Reilly Hall of Temporary Fame, joining such other luminary assistants of the world as:

- Ann Marie, *That Girl* who first put temping and independent living on the map
- Miss Hathaway, who taught us all when we were young that secretaries are smarter than their bosses
- Della Street, Perry Mason's reason for never losing a case
- Elaine, Jerry Seinfeld's friend, who proves that smart, beautiful people can be secretaries, live in New York City, and *still* not have boyfriends
- Carol, Bob Newhart's nail-filing, take-no-grief artiste who ran the office from her reception bay
- Marilyn, Dr. Fleischman's taciturn, guileless, ever-knitting waiting-room Director of Operations
- Miss Moneypenny, M's gatekeeper at the Secret Service and the only woman tough enough to stop James Bond
- Jennifer, the blonde babe who knew more about the radio station *WKRP in Cincinnati* than the manager
- Mia, Dave Barry's Pulitzer Prize–winning secretary
- Agnes, the rhyming, gum-chewing receptionist at the Blue

Moon Detective Agency, taking messages for a *Moonlighting* Maddie and David

◆ Fawn Hall, the Republican pin-up girl, who proved it really does only last fifteen minutes

◆ The Richmeister at the copy machine goofing on the Bossarama

◆ Tonto, who made the phrase, "What do you mean 'we,' *kemo sabe?*" a mantra for sidekicks everywhere

◆ Kato, the original California houseboy chauffeur who karate-kicked ass alongside his *Green Hornet* boss

◆ Alfred, Batman's immaculate confidant and conscience

◆ Benson, who proved you can run any mansion from the kitchen, and of course,

◆ Dr. Watson, the fastidious right arm of the great Sherlock Holmes

Where would the great leaders of our world like the Clampetts and Oliver North be without secretaries and assistants who went so far beyond the call of duty as to actually commit felonies?

It's that kind of effort we're looking for here—hanging off the side of buildings, driving your car over cliffs, smuggling out documents in your underwear. These are the signs of a Temporary Hall of Famer.

Naturally it's any temp's dream to be inducted into Radar's Help Hall, but being of a temporary nature no one's really sure where it's located.

Your First Job of the Day

As a temp, there's no time to warm up. But since you really want to make a good First Impression, for your first job of the day, whatever it is, very carefully proofread your work. Bosses use the method of watching how you perform your first tasks, and then calculate that as a projection of future performance. If you come in letter-perfect in jobs one and two, you can live grief-free for one year. Or several hours, minimum.

The first job's always the hardest, though: You're familiarizing yourself with a new system, typing on a new keyboard, feeling a little under pressure knowing that others will be judging your performance, and you haven't had a chance to warm up to fully functioning computer-secretary mode. Then, on top of that, what if they hand you a massive and complicated document they've been working on for weeks?

Massive Complicated Documents

If you want to protect yourself and take some of the pressure off, copy the complicated document to a duplicate file. By working on this secondary copy, you're relieved of the pressure of screwing up the company's original. Also, if you accidentally delete some command and mess up the format of the rest of the document, you can call up the original and see what went wrong, and/or copy back in the correct commands if you don't know how to do it yourself.

Write a note to copy back or rename the files correctly when done. You'll create widespread panic the next morning if someone retrieves the original file and finds the changes you made yesterday aren't in it. With the note there, even if you walk away from the desk or forget to copy back the document, the first person to come along will see the note and know what to do.

Once you've done all the jobs around the desk and explored every subdirectory and office manual, that's when you can begin easing into your own works/dreams/worlds/books, but I wouldn't recommend too much of it on the first day of your first assignment. See "Advanced Functions" and "Downtime" in chapter 10 after you're sure you haven't been fired and can remember Mmm Mmmm's name for longer than two pages.

Here's a good trick to share with you just to celebrate your first day and all:

The Square Yellow Post-it Trick

You know those little pads of square yellow Post-it stickies? Peel off two of them and stick them together, back-to-back, sticky side at either end so you create a stuck-together square with no sticky outside. This fits conveniently in most pockets and is two-ply for extra strength. It's big enough to use, and not small enough to lose. With a fine point pencil write: the company name (exact spelling), address, zip, phone, fax, any client names and numbers, Mmm Mmmm's name and extension, your extension, nearest coworker's name, who you're replacing, and who you're working for. There are two sides to the double Post-it sticky so you can devise your own system, but this way wherever you roam you'll have all your day's vital information with you.

We'll be going through many other fine office procedures in the upcoming chapters, but here are a few that apply to Opening Day:

Questions

Are you sure you can't figure out the answer yourself? Usually there's a way. Look around you. Information is everywhere.

Never ask bosses, and ask the personnel supervisor only as a last resort. You're supposed to know what you're doing, and bosses don't like to be asked questions, especially stupid ones; they like jobs to be done. Having questions is okay, just direct them to the coworker closest to you who should already be your best friend.

The Exception to Every Rule
You can always ask questions about how printers work. Every printer is different and quirky so questions are expected.

Bosses and Other Aliens

Some people are just real nasty creeps, let's face it. There are people who like to belittle their staff to puff up their own limp noodles. It's an unfortunate thing, but they need a lot more help than you can ever give them in eight hours, so don't even try.

Here are a couple of techniques for dealing with these losers and getting through the day without committing a major crime:

1. Sometimes they'll test you by being short-tempered and put you on the spot to see if you can handle it. Once you pass the test—that is don't talk back, don't start crying, don't draw a blank, but rather complete the task—they respect you and treat you as an equal. So listen. Do what the whiner says. But take careful note to find a hole in their instructions so you can point out how they screwed up when they blame you for doing something wrong, which you know is coming.

2. Some women hate having women work for them and, if you're a woman, you'll have no hope. Some people hate everyone or just particular races or genders. There are plenty of situations in temping where you won't be able to win the person over because of a defect in their DNA. If you do your job and they're still nasty by the afternoon, record the person's name in your files and never come back.

Remember the magic word "counselor." It's appropriate because they counsel us through the trials and tribulations of alien bosses on the job. When you have problems, part of what they're paid to do is talk to you, listen, and help.

You're never alone. The agency is always behind you, and so am I. You can carry me in your bag with all these stress elimination lists and other voodoo-busters. But if you need a human voice, your counselor is your friend. In fact, she's being paid to be your friend. If it's been an awful day and you're almost in tears, call your counselor and pour it out. It's honest, it's being directed toward an employment professional with 911-like experience, and you won't be taking it out on the client or yourself.

Be cool. *You're* not the fool. This ain't school. Temps rule.

The Letterhead Tip-Sheet Trick

This is a good way to remember the places you've been, because if you've done a good job you're likely to be sent back. On your first day at a new assignment, write the following information on a piece of their letterhead. You want to use their letterhead as opposed to blank white paper because the letterhead is designed in such a way as to reflect the culture of the company, it works as a visual memory jogger, and it's a very exact way to keep your notes together with their printed address, phone number, etc. Soon you'll have a file full of letterheads from all the places you've worked with the following handwritten in pencil:

◆ The date and hours you were there
◆ The agency and your rate
◆ Your supervisor on the job
◆ The names of the other people around you
◆ The type of computer and floppy disk drives
◆ The log-in name and password if necessary
◆ Whether you got paid for lunch
◆ Whether there's overtime work
◆ Whether there was a subsidized cafeteria or expensive restaurant
◆ How you got there and how long it took
◆ Some unique item or person that will conjure up the place in your mind
◆ A little floor plan layout of the area with names written in where the people work
◆ Personal impressions and whether you'd want to come back or not

Eventually this collection will give you a written, dated, colorful record of your entire work history. At home, just slip the sheet in your ever-growing Temp folder in either chronological or alphabetical order, and then when you get a call to go somewhere you can check to see if you've been there before and what it was like so you not only know what to expect but can review people's names or bring in a lunch if applicable or be prepared to stay and do overtime because it's that kind of a place.

This way, if the agency calls at eight in the morning and asks if you're available to go in to Greed & Avarice and you think the name rings a bell but aren't sure, you can check your file and realize, "Oh yeah, that's the job from hell." Then you can call back and get out of it on the spot rather than go in and regret it and be in a bad mood all day, probably putting other people in a bad mood, and not creating a good relationship between you and your agency or between the client and the agency. If you know it's bad and can get out of it before it starts—stay home.

The Lunchtime/Halftime Coach's Review

Eat it. But not at your desk. And don't bring in tunafish.

Once you've worked at a place for a while, you can be as strange as they'll let you be. But your first day is a good time to conform to the norm.

You may later choose to skip or shorten lunch. Since most agencies calculate hours in fifteen minute intervals, the shorter the lunch, the higher your pay. Unfortunately, some companies are strict about it and require all employees, including temps, to leave and not be paid for one hour in the middle of the day. This is something that good temps everywhere try to thwart at every assignment. But on your first day, leave for an hour if this is what they want. For one thing, it gives your closest coworker an hour of privacy if you stagger your lunches. This is important to continued good working relations. Plus it gives you an hour to regroup, get distance, breathe fresh air, and plan your afternoon. "Do everything mindfully," as the Buddhists say.

Whether you should subtract one hour for lunch from your timesheet is up to you, but here are a few guidelines: Ask your new best friend working next door to you how strict they are about the lunch hour thing, then conform to the norm. If you've decided you're not coming back to this place again or don't really care about it, go ahead and shoot for the full eight-hour day with no subtraction. If it's a place you want to come back to, scamming that one extra hour might X you out forever and you'd lose thousands of dollars of work in the future.

You should decide by the halftime lunch break whether this is a job you'd like to come back to again. Even if you hate it, don't burn the bridge because it's still the agency you're working for, not the company. Just be nice and coast through the day, neither going above nor much below the line of duty. Do what they say at a steady postal worker's pace with plenty of room to daydream.

If you decide you'd like to work there again, you have the second half of the day to make it a reality. What you want to do is build up a whole repertoire of nice gigs you'd like to play again. It doesn't mean you have to spend the rest of your life at the place, but if you'd like to spend one more day, here's how:

Observe the culture.

The Culture of Offices

The word culture in this case doesn't just mean the cool stuff that inspires your soul, but rather is used in business to describe the overall atmosphere of an office—if it has an international or local flavor; if it's stuffy and uptight or casual and relaxed; if it's creative or regimented; what the dress code is; what the hiring and firing policies are. All of these comprise the culture of the company. But besides the overall attitude, each office has microcultures, which are even more important to notice and adhere to.

The Fable of the Milk and Cookies

True Story Department

I was temping at the Citicorp tower in Queens and every day at exactly three o'clock the entire department came to a stop and everybody went into the kitchen for milk and cookies. I didn't join them the first couple of days because I had other things to do with that downtime, but then all the rest of the day people glared at me. It felt like I was snubbing their religion or something. I didn't realize till the third day what it was, then I started going in for milk and cookies, and they were always nice to me after that!

It just goes to show you—look, listen, and observe the rituals of your microcultures, even if it's not your religion.

Every new job is just a different drama in which the actor in each of us can improvise. The set is built, the characters are established, the plot's in midstream, and you're suddenly in the middle of it. Now, Go!

Have a Sense of Humor or Die

Needless to say, temps can be a repository of some pretty weird tales in an office. Coworkers will confess things to you that they wouldn't tell their best friend because you aren't part of an office clique.

People are stressed out in this world. There have been countless days where I've been sent on a job because I could type but have been retained because I could listen. Sometimes a single quick one-liner can earn you a $100 all-night booking. Just play it light when the stressed-out bosses are getting too heavy. Sometimes all they want is to come out of their office or conference room and have someone who'll laugh at their jokes and tell them everything is fine so they can go back in for four more hours to get torn to shreds by the machetes of greed, and you can go back to your novel.

Comedians and Actors Alert II

You may not be getting paid enough for your skills as a performer now, but employing them in the employment field can earn you the money you're not being rewarded with elsewhere.

Getting Asked Back

In order to get asked back you must distinguish yourself with one or more of the Key Three:

◆ The personnel supervisor
◆ The boss
◆ Your closest coworker

You need to make sure one of them writes down your name.

Connect, interact, jam like you're in Charlie Parker's band. One of the key things employers are looking for in temps is a fresh face to liven up the mood around the old office. You're it. If you're a nice pleasant addition, they'll want you back. If you complain, ask stupid questions you could figure out yourself, talk on the phone, don't pitch in and help, or bring in tunafish, you won't make much money.

The three things personnel supervisors will ask the coworker who was secretly spying on you the whole day are:

◆ Were you a team player? (See "Team Players" in chapter 8 if you need help with this.)

◆ How was your attendance? (Did you stay where you were supposed to, or were you always "in the bathroom" or something?)

◆ How were your phone manners? (Which is code for, did you talk on the phone all day?)

If you can pass those three acid tests, you will *always* be asked back to any job you want to come back to. I personally guarantee it. Tell them you know me.

As long as any one of the Key Three finds some particular positive trait in you, there's reason to call you back. Good help is harder to find than you think. Having read this far in a book you're immediately in the top 10 percent of your class. The average employee in America is so lazy, incompetent, and untrustworthy that even a half-assed effort puts you over the top. Just ask any employment person. Reading a book to improve yourself almost makes you overqualified.

As a last resort, if you haven't been able to connect with any one of the Key Three, your last shot is the person you're filling in for. Leave a funny "Welcome back" or "Hope you're feeling better" type of note and a status report of the work you've completed and where you left things, then sign it with your full name and agency's phone number.

If someone feels their workstation was treated with respect and the person who was replacing them was halfway competent, they'll be inclined to want the same person back instead of taking a chance on someone who leaves tunafish wrappers and long distance phone bills behind.

Remember the permanent secretaries' golden rule: "If you sit here, I don't need a souvenir. Take it with you."

Mission Review

This is a business of relationships; there are two ways to distinguish yourself—with your skills, or with your person. If you can pull both off, you'll work every day you want to for the rest of your life; if you're a little weak in one, you can still win over every job by just playing the other with finesse.

Good luck. It's fun. And don't get stressed.

Remember, you're just a temp.

8

-Making the A-Team-

Now let's get serious. The A-Team is a big secret that most temps don't know about and I'm not even supposed to except I'm from Canada and was an all-star winger on the Eh? Team. In fact this is such a Big Secret that agencies will deny it exists, so don't tell them I told you, but here goes:

Agencies have "A" lists of the temps they send out on jobs first. You want to be on this list. Here's the way it works:

Millions of people walk into temp agencies every day. Some are skilled, some not so skilled. As the agencies fill their job orders, first they send out the skilled ones, but when they're all gone or not available, they're forced to send the scuzzy not-so-skilled ones. Every day that an A-Team all-star knocks 'em dead at the jobsite, the agency's off the hook for a day when Skunky Skidairo knocks 'em out with his freak-man b.o.

If you plan to saddle up to the bar and order a large regular check, you'll need to be a card-carrying A-Team member. But how do you make it? Even if you read all the way to the end of this book and back again it doesn't guarantee you a spot. And you can't bribe your way onto it, though Lord knows I've tried. Why? Because this is the bread and butter team of every agency.

So here's every tip in the book for making *The Team*. First up →

Don't Get N.G.s *or* You'll End Up At D.N.U.

The first goal is: don't get "N.G.s." In the employment biz "N.G." stands for "Not Good." If you get a complaint about you for any reason from a client you'll get an "N.G." beside your name for that assignment. If you get more than about two of these you won't likely be sent out by that agency again. You can get them even when you don't deserve them, but if that's the case and you have an open, honest relationship with your counselor, they'll believe you and either delete it from your file or add a note to explain it.

If you get enough N.G.s you can apply to D.N.U.—that vulnerable institution of lower losing, Dumb Nuts University, accepting applicants from temp agencies all across the country who have failed so miserably on the job that they are branded in scarlet across their forehead—**D**o **N**ot **U**se.

Don't be branded—be candid. Tell your counselor when you're at a bad assignment and give her the specifics so your side is represented and you don't get some bad initials without a fair defense.

But not getting N.G.s only keeps you off the bottom. How do you swim through the middle and come out on top?

Collecting Rave Reviews

You need to distinguish yourself. You need to perform so over-and-above the call of duty that a client compliments you to the agency. You need to be so super-friendly and competent on the jobsite that when your agency calls to see how it's going they just rave about you—this way you actually get a "Good" in your file beside the job assignment. If you collect a few of these in the first ten or twenty assignments, you'll be a regular on the A-Team in no time.

If you feel that you've aced the day or have any kind of a good relationship at all with the personnel supervisor, when she says anything resembling, "Good job," or "You did good," or "We'd like to have you back," train yourself to leap right in with the phrase, "Let them know at the agency." If you can get those few words to flow right off the end of her sentence she'll fall in with, "Yeah, I will." Boom d'dee boom. It's a perfectly natural conversational segue you can trigger with a well-timed "Let-them-know" line.

Sometimes the personnel person will leave before you get a chance to see her, or will be too busy when you come by, or, even though you've worked hard enough to warrant a rave review, it just doesn't happen. You might bust your butt, but the client is so busy with other things they forget to mention how good you were. Don't be discouraged. Just do the same thing next time and soon the karmic slot-machine of Temp City will come up flush and drown you in coinage. K'ching!

The agency knows how rare an actual compliment out of a client is, so it only takes a couple of these to put you on the A-Team.

The second best alternative to a rave review is to leave a good impression and your name on a piece of paper so when the company calls to order another temp they'll have a record of your name and ask for you. One request from a client is worth twenty words-per-minute on a typing test—so if you can't score one way, you can always score another. I think Bob Seger said that.

Getting Yourself Booked Back

When an agency sends you on a job and you end up getting yourself booked back without the agency having to do any work— that's another way on to the A-Team. If you go out on an eight-hour day and bring home a week's worth of bacon, you've just earned the agency a mound of dough they didn't know was in the oven, and now the two of you can split the bread. They appreciate these little touches.

Just after you finish doing something particularly well and can see a smile in response, ask the person you're working for at the jobsite, "Hey, are you going to be needing anyone the rest of the week?" If you can pull off the question while the smile's still in bloom you've got the best chance of the day for a positive response. Or you can pull the old "Catching the 5:25," where you pop the overtime question just when everybody else is leaving but you know he'll be needing help. For more precise directions on perfecting this trick, turn to "Milking the Cows."

You can also make the A-Team just by remembering Mmm Mmmm's name. You can make it by being friends with every candy striper on the floor. You can make it by accidentally-on-purpose bumping into Mmm Mmmm during the day, and tossing out one of those irresistible work-inducing one-liners, such as: "Oh hi! Hey, what's going on for the rest of the week?" or "Want to keep things consistent?" or "I'm available through Friday."

If it's your first day, I recommend the always popular, "It's a nice atmosphere here." This says to them you feel at home and prompts the very easy rejoinder, "You'll be back."

If you're returning to a site you've conquered before, I've found the greeting, "Good to see you again," prompts the "Yeah, good to see you too" comeback, positively reinforcing the vibe of YOU.

Go slow. Be calm. Be yourself. Make friends.

Flexibility

Be a Gumby. Temping is an imprecise art and a lot of different people, moods, and circumstances are involved in its creation. Nothing ever happens the same way twice. Three independent forces—the client who orders God-knows-who to show up and work at their company, the agency who sends some once-interviewed stranger to do the work of the client who keeps them in business, and the temp who could be sent to Frankenstein's laboratory for a midnight experiment—collide on a daily basis in a place we call the Temping Zone. It's pretty much a miracle that any of this ever works at all.

That's why Gumby-like flexibility is such a valued commodity. If you can bend—work sometimes when you don't really want to, stay later than you were booked, sometimes all night, or be nice about a cancellation at the last minute—suddenly you make that long-odds gamble less risky for all.

If you bend a few times and the agency sees you're flexible and they can count on you, you're on the A-Team.

But remember this Warning Reminder: You're in charge of your time now. Although you want to be available and flexible to make the A-Team, don't fall into the trap of feeling that you must accept every assignment that comes along or you'll be losing one of the key benefits of being a temp in the first place—freedom. Refer back to "Tools" in the "First Steps" chapter and get yourself a phone machine and a phone with a ringer you can turn off.

Working is important—but not working is essential.

Reliability

The percentage of temps who screw up is astoundingly high. You wouldn't believe some of the stories about people who have been sent out on jobs and simply not shown up. The counselor assumes the temp will be there, the client is notified, the temp is expected, the whole world is on hold, but the temp just goes right back to sleep. Meanwhile the boss is tapping his finger and the personnel supervisor is assuring him the temp is on the way because the temp agency has assured the supervisor. People are waiting on the other side of the globe for the work to be done and the contracts to be e-mailed so a faltering business that employs twenty thousand people on three continents can stay afloat and the temp just lies back down on his pillow and goes to sleep.

Boy, did I get in trouble for that one! But these kinds of stories happen every single day in Templand. And they give counselors nightmares every single night. The point is, reliability is fairly high up on their criteria scale.

A lot of people don't even seem to know what reliability means anymore, so here's what it says in *The Official Temps' Dictionary:*

> **reliability** *(noun)* Doing what you say you're going to do; never letting people down; being where you say you'll be, and staying there; accepting job assignments when you say you're available.

You need to be able to trust your agency when they describe a job they're sending you to. You want them to send you to fun and profitable places on a regular basis. You want your agency to be reliable, so you be reliable. In fact, you'll be *relying* on them for your income.

One of the fastest ways to the A-Team is treating your agency with the same respect with which you wish to be treated. If you're not a lightning typist or computer wiz, you can still make the A-Team with honesty, reliability, and respect. (Listen to Aretha Franklin if you're still having problems with any of this.)

Team Players

A team player is someone who pitches in, does more than his or her share, doesn't mind answering someone else's ringing phone, takes some overflow work if there's downtime, or runs an errand if someone else is swamped.

People who think their own square cubicle is their only responsibility are not team players. People who are out for their own fame and glory are not team players. You can recognize team players by looking at where the metaphor began: team sports. Athletes who leap from team to team every few years are not "team players." The ones who stick with the team and build a tradition, giving more of themselves than is expected, are team players.

Team players recycle paper and other things; non–team players do not. Team players volunteer to help others; non–team players only look out for themselves. Team players ask those around them what time it would be convenient for them to take lunch; non–team players just walk out without asking. Team players know what comes around goes around; non–team players have not heard the song "Instant Karma."

Getting along with people is no longer an optional skill. Every encounter from the moment you call the agencies in the very first rounds to how you perform on the job today, is a short test of your interpersonal skills. Some people are better at this than others, but all of us can always improve because each day is a series of little tests that allow us to see how people are responding to us. Every human interaction, from dropping a coin in the slot as you board a bus to ordering a sandwich, is a chance for you to test and practice your interpersonal skills.

One of the things that temping forces us to do is integrate. If you do this well enough you'll become a team player. And if you get really good at it, eventually you'll become a team leader.

Smile. Be nice to people. It's one of the perks of living.

Overflow

Overflow is a term used in offices to describe the work that needs to be done when one or more of the secretaries gets flooded with more work than she'll be able to accomplish in the time frame allotted. The secretary will then call the personnel supervisor and ask for help with the "overflow" of work she's got. The personnel supervisor then calls around to find a secretary who isn't very busy and asks her to help clean up the overflow mess. This is a very common practice of work redistribution.

One of the best ways to win A-Team membership is to call the personnel supervisor when things are quiet and offer to help with overflow. The more you do this, the more the personnel supervisor will like you, and the more she likes you, the more likely she'll ask for you back and the more likely you'll have a starting position on the A-Team.

You should also be aware of overflow for your own sake. If you've temped at a company for a while and they know you're capable of an honest day's work, you're as eligible as a regular secretary to call the personnel supervisor and advise her you're overwhelmed and won't be able to accomplish everything by the end of the day. If what you're saying is true, you even get added brownie points for accurately assessing the situation and taking the appropriate measures. It's worse to get to the end of the day and not have done all the work that's expected to be done than it is for you to call in and ask for help. You don't want to make a habit of it, but if you need help, ask for it.

Please heed this one warning about calling the personnel supervisor with your availability to help with overflow: *Never do it in front of other secretaries.* Three reasons: 1) it looks like you're kissing up to the boss and no one respects that even if everyone does it; 2) it looks bad for the person you're filling in for because it suggests she isn't being given enough work to do on a regular basis because here you are doing her job and you've still got time to spare; and 3) the other secretary who hears you call in will start funneling her work to you if she thinks you're so un-busy as to be actually *looking* for work and effectively squealing on her normal work partner. So the best advice is to wait until your secretarial baymate is taking a break away from her desk before calling in your overflow availability, or take a stroll past the supervisor's office and tell her in person.

Every Desk Organizing Trick in the World

This section applies only to long-term assignments, neutral office floater desks, and new assignments where your desk is *not* someone else's home away from home.

Let's say your skills are up, your typing's good, you're being pleasant, hard working, and you're winning over your neighbors, but what about maximizing your actual work station? What can you do at your desk that can make you an even better performer?

SURFING GENERAL'S WARNING: Cigarettes kill you. But also, don't mess with the desk. If you're at another person's desk for a day, besides leaving it clean, the main thing is not to disturb the settings on her computer, keyboard, or seat. They'll even be able to tell if you flipped a postcard over and read it. As SuperAgent Sandy says, "Crumbs on the desk is one of the quickest ways to an N.G."

If it's actually your desk, you have an opportunity to earn A-Team distinction by showing off the greatest organization in the office and producing your work the quickest. The reason is the Law of Exactitude: the more exact you are, the better you do things. Because work—both your own and other people's—will be flying across your desk and nothing but your desk so help you God, you'd better keep it clean and calibrated to top torqueage.

You must have all of your tools in perfect working order, on the surface, and in plain view. You must have multiple backups of every tool in a drawer within reach of your desk. You must have your utensils separated in different jars—one for pencils, one for ball-point pens, one for highlighters, one for felt pens, one for rulers, scissors, nail files & miscellaneous—just as a for-instance to get you started. Expand as needed.

The inside of pencil jars must be kept perfectly clean and free of ink pens because they leak. The pencils should all be pointed up with the erasers on the bottom to keep them free from graphite. This preserves the integrity of the erasers below and the sharpness of the point above. There should be strict penalties for violation of this rule.

All pens, regardless of color, sex, or creed, should point downward because that's the way the ink flows. Storing a pen with the tip toward heaven causes the ink to drip to hell, creating one for the user.

Those occasional inkless white-outs in the middle of your sentences are caused by some homicidal maniac who stored the pen upside down. This rule of earthward ink flow has been in effect since that other great clerical worker Galileo got pissed off and started throwing things out his window.

If the company doesn't have multiple paperclip holders, the boxes the paperclips come in make perfectly good containers. Just cut the top off then tape it once around the perimeter to hold it together. Get used to making instant assessments of the size required between large and small; always have plenty of both on hand; and recycle the incoming into the appropriate container. The right-sized clip is like tying the perfect bow on a birthday present.

Always have a large stack of napkins within reach of your seat for emergency spills or cleaning. You spend more time at this spot than anywhere except bed so you may as well keep it clean just for the health of it.

Without Moving Your Butt

The following should be within reach of your seat. First, the desk—there's really no point sitting out in the middle of nowhere, so you should slide in near a desk. Then you'll want your phone, computer, and printer; the paper supply, including blank, letterhead, and second page; a pile of scrap paper to reuse; a recycling receptacle; all dictionaries and office manuals; stacks of pads to write on; blank manila folders; all those pen and pencil jars; the mail box; the In-box and the Out-box; a Sideways-box just to confuse the mailroom guy; a picture of your Sweetie.

The Martha Stewart Segment

If the office doesn't have enough of those pen jars I alluded to, a soup can can do the job. Use a can-opener to cut the top right off. Make sure there isn't a sharp edge on the inside; use a screw driver or spoon or any steel thing to flatten out the little sharp edge if there is one. Peel off the paper label, wash the can real well, and while it's drying flip through your favorite magazine to look for a picture of your favorite celebrity, outdoor scene, or other image you like to look at. Once the can is completely dry, wrap the picture around it like a new label using transparent tape to seal it where the paper comes together on the back. Now you've got your own person-alized, perfect-size pen-holder with your favorite person or painter brightening your workday.

` Be Perfect but Not a Perfectionist

I've seen a lot of healthy young temps shot down their first day because they overedit, overperfect, overtweak, and double-check everything twice.

It's nice to be precise, but it's more precise to be nice. Observe the weather pattern: If it's a sunny day and you've only got one letter to type, then you can proofread it a second time to check its layout and make sure it's letter-perfect (ha-ha) before handing it in. But if it's stormy weather with incoming wounded, then you need to fly and turn the job around in five minutes and hand it back to him with your left hand as you begin the next with your right while fielding a phone call on your shoulder and an outgoing fax on your lap.

If you're a compulsive Felix Unger who's got to have everything ironed and folded, you'd better prepare yourself for Oscar now. War and business are messy affairs, and if you can't handle the sight of gushing paper cuts and fired employees with flowing tears, you better keep out of the bull ring, Bucko.

The Old Mission-Impossible-Secret-Dossier Routine

If you're returning to a place you've been before and it's somewhere you want to become a regular, bring in the piece of letterhead that you started your first day and have modified on each subsequent visit. If you want to make the A-Team and play here more than occasionally you'll need to take this tip-sheet idea to a whole other level. We're talking an entire manila folder, creating *an entire dossier* containing every angle and fact available on the place you want to work. I don't know anybody else who does this, so it'll definitely set you above the pack. Or get you committed.

Turn the outside of the manila folder into your quick-scan cheat sheet by writing down the really vital data that you need in the flash of an eye, such as how to transfer a call, the secretarial supervisor's name, the telephone code to pick up the phones at night, etc.

Now, here's the really exciting part: fill up the file with all sorts of cool secrets and maps and facts that allow you to have access to everything when you return so you don't have to ask a single question but have the complete layout of the company, including access to the computers and every person's name.

The reason you're assembling this file—a process which takes place over time and never stops evolving—is because you may not go back to this same company for months, but when you do, you'll now be armed with as much of the following information as you can gather on each visit:

◆ Your letterhead page with the correct name, address, phone, and fax numbers.

◆ Your rates for the different shifts at this particular company, plus your agency's phone number, and payroll schedule.

◆ All the little square yellow Post-its you've made on prior visits.

◆ A copy of the company's complete telephone directory; use a highlighter to mark everyone you know or places you need to dial while working there. If you're at a company with hundreds of employees, by highlighting the names of the people you meet, you begin to scratch the surface of the maze of names and to develop contacts in the small city you've just moved into.

◆ Complete telephone instructions for transferring calls, getting an outside line, retrieving voice mail messages, etc. Often these are printed for guests on a single sheet of paper and you can just photocopy it.

◆ Copies of any instructions you gather for how to use the fax machine, make coffee, call local messenger services or overnight couriers, or order masseuses.

◆ Notes on specific procedures at the company, like how concerned they are with punctuality, what you do with your lunch hour, whether their dress code includes casual Fridays, etc. Since every business has its own quirks, the dossier is the best way to keep the different customs straight.

◆ A floor plan with all the rooms and offices labeled; these are often given out as office guides that employers print for their new employees or guests. Ask for one if you don't see one—it shows you're taking an interest in doing things right. If you can't secure a preprinted floor diagram, draw your own, marking who sits where and all the places you visit so in the future you'll know who you've met and where you've been.

◆ A computer cheat sheet including: how-to reference guides for the programs you use at that company; a list of macros that are unique to that company; all the computer access names and passwords you garner in your exploits, because you never know when you might need some unconventional way into the network when all other methods fail. For those of you who don't do Windows, it's a good idea to keep a copy of the standard DOS Character Codes Chart that lists the special characters you can create by using Ctrl-V and a combination of numbers.

◆ An extra blank diskette, because, hey, you never know.

◆ Several timesheets from your agency.

◆ Night codes and employee numbers for access to computers or doors if you work the graveyard shift, so you don't get stuck in some tiny hallway and have to wait there for three hours until the delivery guy drops off the bagels about six in the morning.

◆ Home phone numbers of all cute guys (or babes) and other important people.

◆ Take-out restaurant menus and food-source phone numbers and their hours.

◆ Notes to yourself of your impressions of the place and how to milk their cows.

◆ Notes on who's naughty and nice.

◆ A copy of the Temp Commandments located at the rear of this book.

◆ Inspirational quotes from Jesus or Jerry or whoever gets you through the night so you're traveling with your own personal scripture whenever you need deliverance from evil, for there is the power, and the glory, for ever and ever, whoa man!

You don't need every single one of those things in each and every folder, but all of them will come in handy and it creates a comfort zone from which you can operate. It's like your own personalized textbook to refer back to. Regular full-time employees who work there internalize this data. If you want to be a valuable A-Team temp and not a beast of burden, the *Mission Impossible* Secret Dossier Folder can give you the same knowledge as a regular without taking up any of your own personal hard disk space.

Getting to Know Them From the Front Carpeting

This is sort of an advanced function feature, but I think you're about as advanced as I am functional at this point, so just don't spill anything.

There are only so many different types of jobs. After doing this a while, you can begin to tell what a job is like from the lobby carpeting, e.g.: If it's new and rich brown and looks like hardly anybody's ever walked on it, the atmosphere of the office will be quiet, the equipment will be new, you won't be too busy but you'll have to be very precise, not talk on the phone, and keep a low profile.

If the carpet's new but with more primary colors such as red or green, the office will be busy, up-tempo, there'll be a lot of work but it will get done quickly, both men and women will be chipper and flirtatious, lunch hour will be long and unsupervised, and you can probably get away with working on your screenplay as long as you also fly through the required work. Not much work will be done after 4 P.M. except by the nerdy guy who pushed for the darker carpets.

If it's gray and worn near the door, turn around and go home. Anybody who buys gray carpeting probably hasn't bought a new computer since the Apple Seedling, which they're still convinced works perfectly fine, thank you. If it's worn by the door, there probably isn't going to be free coffee or much else. If the worn-out track continues past a vacant reception desk, there are too few people doing too much work, and you probably won't be inquiring about their pension plan.

If it's worn down the middle but shows signs it was once a floral or geometric pattern, there's going to be tons of work to do but no one's really going to care if it gets done or not, and as long as you get *something* done, you can also use switch-screen and work on your own stuff.

And you can take these gems to the bank.

If you can practice your own internal process of assessing what's before you, and adapting to it before it comes to pass, you can forever turn the slivers of hardwood into the red carpet treatment.

Making the A-Team is the same as winning over any other person or group. Adapt, be prepared, be polite, be proud of yourself, be flexible, reliable, honest, and straightforward. Make committed eye contact and do what you're asked.

If you end up at a place you don't like, you don't have to go back tomorrow. But for the one day you're there, be *all* there. Don't walk out on an angry client. Do not take that one parting shot. Tell your friends you did if you have to, but don't actually do it. Just do your job, leave, and never go back.

If it's a place you decide you like, study its particulars, memorize its players, and blend in like a complementary addition. Two or three key clients and you can be comfortably employed for the rest of your life. Please enjoy.

Closings and Candy Bars

Closings: Just the sound of the word sends shivers up some secretaries' spines. If you're planning to work in the high-paying specialty fields of legal or executive, you'll soon find out why. This is the hardest, most intense time in Templand. A lot of people don't even know what closings are, so I'll play you the hoedown:

Closings are the ends of deals that you're working on all the rest of the time. Closings are the same as when you go and buy any product from a candy bar to a house. The moment when the money actually changes hands is the completion, or "closing" of the deal.

When you buy a candy bar and hand the man 50¢, you're agreeing to hand over the sum of 50¢ under the assumption and agreement that you'll be satisfied with the yummy little bundle of chocolate and goo. You may hem and haw a little bit more about the purchase of a new stereo, so it becomes a little bit bigger deal. You can probably remember the moment you bought your last home entertainment unit because you exchanged a substantial percentage of your gross worth for a digital thing with too many buttons on it. If you take this to an even higher level, think about how much people freak out over buying a house—so much so they actually talk to lawyers. But if you just think of a house as a very large bundle of chocolate and goo, you'll realize why people like to buy property.

Well, closings in business are like really, really huge aircraft-carrier-sized candy bars that cost billions of dollars, in case you're wondering how we got into debt. So if you remember how much you sweated over that puny stereo, imagine big merger closings where some corporate aircraft carrier is engulfing some poor chocolate dinghy in a single gulp. That will give you an idea of the tension between the guy who's doing the billion dollar gulp and the goo ball that's about to get swallowed.

It makes for some pretty tense showdowns. They argue all year, sometimes for many years, about the exact details of the deal, without feeling much pressure because they were just yelling at each other over conference-call speakerphones. Once they actually set a date for the closing and the combatants fly in from all over the world and actually get in the same room together for the transaction with only a few days left to fight over it, things get kind of hairy. And there you are, innocent little screenplay writer just looking for a few quiet hours in front of a terminal, but it turns out you're in at a closing and all these poor lawyers are losing years off their lives right in front of you. You're forced to witness suicide by ulcer and murder by greed and there's nothing you can do about it except write a book called *The Firm* and bilk them out of as many hours as possible while their eyes are raging like rabid dogs.

Although it's true that some closings can be amicable deals where both sides are happy, that only accounts for about one in four. Half of them are tense for only the final twenty-four hours as one of the parties is killed off. The fourth of the four will be a monster clash between two Goliaths who aren't about to budge, or some little David who is out to prove himself and isn't giving an inch. Quite often these combatants have been trained in law school (long hours), then became young associates at law firms (longer hours), and are now in the bucking-for-partner phase (longest hours), because once they become partner they have (no hours).

What happens is, the combatants pick a time for the transfer of funds to take place. Since nobody really owns corporations except for banks located all over the world including Tokyo, all of these institutions have to agree that at a certain time on a certain day all these different piles of hundreds of millions of dollars will change hands, so that's the day everybody has to have all their pennies in a line. Funds have to be cleared, clauses and numbers have to be finalized, and then *boom!* the magic hour chimes and the money begins a series of wire transfers among different bank accounts all over the world. Once all of these wire transfers are completed, the closing is completed, and the Giant Corporation may now eat the candy bar.

I hope that was perfectly clear.

The part where you come in is: you sit outside the ring (conference room) and between rounds your fighter stumbles out and hands you revisions to the contract they're dying over.

This is the most intense time in Templand, and only the best need apply. It requires a high skill level, plus a high tolerance for taking insults from arrogant weasels, all the while performing the work of six people, remembering everything including names, and always being pleasant. Oftentimes, one secretary (you) will be the only person revising the contracts, and both sides will burst out of different doors of the same conference room and throw stuff at you at the same time demanding it be "done right now and perfectly because if I see one more mistake in this thing we're walking away from the deal."

You have to coolly disregard everything except for the "do this now" part, make sure you're clear on the task, words, notes, edits, orders, and proceed with haste. Make eye contact. Understand instructions and write them down immediately. Mark the documents you'll be handling with Post-it notes and brief instructions or descriptions. If you're given numerous tasks, all of which are "priority," ask in which order they should be completed so that you're following traceable directives. Never say to a frantic person in the middle of a closing that you can't do something. As long as you understand the instructions, you can find out how to do it later.

If there's one thing you should remember at a closing it's that the anger expressed toward you is never to be taken personally. This is just a job. You're just a temp. Even if they're yelling at you and implying you're doing a bad job, they're not really yelling at you. There are seven thousand things wrong in their lives and in the ring and you're just the latest slugger in the punchline. <<Web link to "Coping Strategies" in the next chapter.>>

The golden benefit that compensates for the stressful moments of a closing is the week leading up to it. This is when you often get hardcore downtime because they need to have secretarial support on hand for the moment the paper explodes and everybody goes crazy, so they're willing to pay a temp to be sitting at-the-ready at the computer. There could be *days* of quiet. Days and days. And generally when I get about a week to myself at the top dollar, I don't mind doing the work of ten men on the last day. *K'boom!*

Playing in the Pocket

What you want to do is get *inside* the deal, get a sense of the other players around you: their tempo, rhythm, pace, humor, ability, intelligence, personality. This way you can anticipate—you can "be"—on the inside.

Here's how to prepare:

- Do the whole desk preparation outlined earlier.
- Have all your tools and equipment in perfect working order.
- Fill the printer with paper, fill the desk with supplies, let your agency and supervisor know your extension, and familiarize yourself with the documents on the computer.
- Scan through the main pledge agreement, or whatever central document they're working on to brush up on any functions that you aren't real familiar with.
- Familiarize yourself with the "players" or "working group" lists of all participants in the deal; ask your nearest support staff who the key players are and highlight their names.
- Make sure the coffee is made and you're drinking some.

Coffee Time

Perhaps it's time to deal with coffee and other explosives.

It gets pretty hairy around those desks and papers. When closings hit their peak, pads, proposals, and prospectuses are tossed around like Frisbees on a beach. Paper cups of brown liquid are not exactly the movable objects you want to encounter in this very hard place. One spill at the wrong time and you—and maybe a whole deal—goes down the drain. Ploosh tip gloosh and you've got Carl Lewis running wild all over your desktop, and the attorney who hasn't slept since last Sunday and is mildly stressed out looks down and sees his red-felt notes washing away in a sea of stupidity and he drops to the floor in an epileptic fit of despair, clutching his chest just before dying.

Seen it a million times. If you can't balance a coffee while riding a bicycle through traffic, curb your drinking at the peak of the closing.

Be a Free Toaster

Now let's return to the task of preparing your desk with the care of a drummer tuning his kit before a show. Sharpen your pencils, assemble extra notepads and Post-its, understand everything around you, sort piles of papers so you're ready when the conference room doors finally fly open and lawyers tear out of there like bargain hunters at a door-opening sale where you're the only free toaster!

There'll be a rush for a while and you'll be really busy, then all of a sudden they'll get sucked back into their conference room void and the doors will slam in harmony and all will be totally silent like an empty concert hall at midnight.

Closings often go on for days on end, 'round the clock with nary a break. There are two ways you can play it: run the whole streak, known as the "SuperTemp Play," or else pick one of the three eight-hour cycles and lock in a booking through the end of the deal.

Many times the quietest shift on a closing is the graveyard shift (midnight–8 A.M., so-named because that's where you'll end up if you try to work then and still have a day life). Sometimes the evening shift (5 P.M.–midnight) is the quietest because it's transition time, when the players are all talking and eating dinner and not under the pressure of the day, but by 11:00 or 12:00 they've stopped chattering and start churning out real work and you'll want to get out of there as soon as possible. It's a gamble, but you can make an educated guess once you get on a deal and watch its flow.

The goal, of course, is to get paid, fed, and put in a car home after several hours of doing nothing but your own stuff. Closings often need people standing by for days on end and I don't mind sitting in. Sometimes you get stuck and actually have to do some work, but by now you should know how to handle that.

It's one of those "work really hard or not at all," rather than one of those "work a little bit all the time" routines. You may be shooting for the times when it's quiet, but you'll have to work really hard when it's not. Otherwise you won't last.

Closings are the time to become Octopusman—the eight-armed master who battles the evils of attorneys while simultaneously creating new documents and paper-clipping the last batch while handing out messages to the suit walking past and photocopies to the skirt standing still while asking, "What's this word here?" to the young one walking away, and "Did you want that duped to a new version or should I make changes to the current?" to the nice one, and, "Hello, conference room," into the phone with a nod of acknowledgment while taking in fresh changes to the Loan Agreement while writing down the name of the person being sought by the caller from Singapore.

Let's Review

Distinguish yourself from the pack by being the best; book yourself back; team players are always in the game; practice Radar O'Reilly by day and sing Aretha Franklin by night; if you keep your paper clips separated, your paper will take care of itself; keep a secret dossier on every place that's keeping one on you; don't forget the floor plan; take careful note of the carpeting; play in the pocket, be in love with your own life, and remember—when the Weasel is yelping, it's never at you.

9

-Survival Techniques-

Inevitably all good things seem to come to an end, or at least they do in my case, and you end up getting a lousy assignment—one of those gray carpet deals.

Those so inclined can find a lot of reasons to use temps for target practice, so if you want to survive in the highly competitive world of out-of-work secretaries you'd better know how to suffer the slings and arrows of outrageous abuse. Although, truthfully, you don't see slings the way you used to.

The PHAST Track

The best technique for shielding yourself from incoming missiles is with some "Polite, Honest, And Straightforward Talking," or PHAST for short. By disarming your opponent with honesty in the opening round, you seize the power for the day. Here's how:

Step One: Throw your coffee in his face and go, "Oh yeah?!"

No, I'm kidding. That works less often than you'd like it to.

Try this: Disarm the offending party by questioning him, but in a really deferential way. For instance, if his voice is a little loud and angry and you can hear it's being perceived that way around you, say loud enough for everyone to hear, "Is something wrong?" He immediately realizes he's acting as though something is—when nothing is. Or if something *is*, he'll say it and you'll resolve the matter with witnesses.

If the hothead's expecting you to know things you couldn't possibly know, say, "I'm sorry sir, this is my first day, and I've just about got it down, but what about...(whatever part is most particularly unclear)."

If he's giving you more than two things to do at once and talking really fast and expecting you to catch every detail, speak up early and ask questions to break his flow. With each new task he gives you, ask, "Now, where does this go in the sequence?" Use your words in a proactive way at the beginning to break his rapid fire and establish a groundwork for your eight-hour relationship.

Coping Strategies

Although most on-the-job problems can be solved quickly by PHAST communication, some problems originate within your head and are best resolved in there.

The most common on-the-job complaint from temps is that they're belittled, made to feel subservient, insulted, or yelled at for no reason. You must remember the condescending attitude directed toward you has nothing to do with you and is only a temporary by-product of a temporary situation that you arrived late to and will be leaving early from.

The problem of being yelled at or made to feel subservient at a full-time job is much more complex and destructive to the soul and psyche because the recipient doesn't know which of his or her thousands of actions and statements are combining to produce the insults or reprimand being received. Added to this is the pressure that the complaint or degradation may adversely affect your long-term career—and even your financial security.

As a temp, these factors are permanently removed from the equation. You're no longer surrounded by people who are going to share your career for life; you're employed beyond the place where the temporary stress is taking place; and most importantly, what-ever condescending or otherwise offensive personal trait your office assailant is exhibiting, it all began long before you got there.

Reread the "Chilling-Out Rules" in chapter 3 if you need a refresher of the mantras to get over it, but in a larger sense, in order to cope with this world full of angry people bitter over their shake of the dice, it's easier when you see them as only a temporary distraction. It's your choice whether you return tomorrow. There are lots of ways to respond to nasty people, but one of the easiest is to call your counselor and let her know you're not coming back.

During the moment when Evil Person is standing in front of you wailing away about some such nonsense, completely zone out his words by filling your mind with the questions, "I wonder what it is that makes him this way? Is it resentment over someone else having a life? Maybe a parent who beat him? Or a lover who left him? Never having a lover? Tight underwear? Tight fisted?" By the time you've run through your multiple-choice options the idiot has stopped babbling and you missed the whole thing. Presto! Instant peace! Take your brain, add water, and ignore the weeds.

Other techniques to remember from the outset:

◆ This isn't going to hurt your career.
◆ This isn't going to affect the way you make a living.
◆ This isn't based on anything you said or did.
◆ You never have to lay eyes on this person again.
◆ What if you were married to this person?
◆ Could you imagine?

And then start singing, "People, who hate people, are the loneliest people, in the world."

If you're still having a tough time letting insults roll off, read

The Umbrella Story

Bad things happening are like rainstorms: They'll always happen, and the rain will fall on everyone equally. There's no avoiding the rains of misfortune, but what you can do is put up an umbrella so you don't get wet.

The umbrella is the coping mechanism that works best for you. Whether it's Born Again Christianity, happy Buddhism, kind budism or humming the songs of the Grateful Dead, the key is carrying your own mental umbrella of protection with you everywhere.

The rains will still fall all around you. Other people will get soaked and angry and bogged down in the puddles of their own despair. Some will run around like chickens looking for the nearest canopy for shelter. But the cool cats are carrying an emotional umbrella for all-day protection against the rains of eternity. They're able to just pop that black 'brella open and keep on moving forward without missing a beat.

One of the reasons temping is such a holy calling is because it teaches its young to become helpful healers. In no time you'll be fixing someone's broken document like a surgeon, and when they see you do it they'll think it's a miracle and be forever grateful. These are the rewards that give your umbrella support.

The next day you may tackle a job that looked nearly impossible and not only pull it off, but add that extra zing and make it sing. These moments, too, become the supports of your umbrella.

It will always be raining somewhere in the world. Someone will always be having a bad day, bad luck, or bad breath when they least expect it. You can teach yourself to use your umbrella and stay dry so you can keep moving in the direction you were going before the rains hit—or you can stand and wait under an awning with the Complaining People for the rest of your life.

Troublesome Temps and Other Coworkers to Avoid

The complex process of surviving the day involves not only repelling repugnant bosses but avoiding dangerous temps and lethal regulars as well. Here are some Advance Warning Lights of the hull-shearing reefs you'll want to steer clear of:

The Snitch

Hard to detect. Since you need to interact with your closest coworkers, and Snitches are so hard to spot until it's too late, the best advice is to not say or admit anything that could be taken the wrong way. Follow the lead of the other workers around you and monitor their relationships with one another. Snitches do not have friends-a-plenty around the office. If the coworker closest to you seems like the nicest person in the world, make sure other people in the office are coming by and treating her that way too. Sometimes the nicest people are really the smoothest con-artist-snitches who are picking your pocket of secrets and you don't even know it. Since you're new, the Snitch has every advantage over you, so the best test is the old Other-Worker-as-a-Mirror routine, where you watch the expression of those facing your potential Snitch. If your nearest coworker doesn't have regular visitors with regular smiles, beware of the bear and don't get caught in the snare.

The Gossip

Easier to detect than the Snitch because she never shuts up. The key to spotting the Spotted Gossip is the incessant questions. Gossips are like wild animals feeding—and you're the news they live on. If you're a big ripe fruitcake they're going to gorge on you until the end of the day and even chase you all the way to the elevator to get in one last bite. Every morsel of information will be twisted around by the Gossip's vivid imagination and added to other things from outer space to create phantasmagorical stories starring you! And these exploitation films are not going to win you an Oscar, so beware. Do Not Feed the Animals. (Also comes in medium, large, and male.)

The Comedian

Usually male. Key clue: Always trying too hard. Dangerous by association. The Comedian is always trying to win you and everyone else within earshot over in a nonstop monologue. Beware. Comedians annoy upper management because it's always showtime and they're rarely seen doing any actual work. And when the show gets busted, everybody goes down, including the audience. Remember: they saw you coming long before you saw them, and they've been playing you like a violin since breakfast. Once you spot them, listen from a distance with your back turned so you can enjoy the solo without being sucked into the jam. Once they find somebody to play with they never let go. Be smart. Don't start.

The Blabbermouth

Like the others, except without an agenda. Doesn't talk to gain gossip. Doesn't talk to put people down. Just talks. And talks. And you're sitting there wondering, "Is she talking to me or on the phone or what?" Unlike Snitches who are hard to spot, and Comedians who sneak up on you, Blabbermouths are obvious by about 9:03. They're also dangerous by association because they're noticed by personnel and management as nonworkers and if you respond to their opening salvos they'll distract you from your work. They're usually low on skills and self-esteem. Like Comedians, they're highly flammable. Once ignited they're difficult to extinguish, and if you're nearby, you will get burned. Best defense: The sidebag I suggested in the "Tools" section that includes your eight hours of personal projects. Immediately open up your own work and bury yourself PHAST: "Is that so? Well I never. Listen, this is really interesting, but I have to get something finished before tomorrow." And never tell them a thing about what you're working on because a) they'll talk to you about it until the end of the day, and b) they'll talk to everyone else about it until the end of the century.

The Magazine Flipper

Also causes guilt by association. Dangerous because it looks like the entire bay area where you and Flipper are swimming is not busy and that work should be directed your way. Best defense: Be actively typing and working on the computer to make it look like you're busy in contrast to Flipper, whether it's your work or the company's. In fact, some Radarians have been known to actually type the same sentence over and over when the Bossman is walking past just to look like they're doing work so that they avoid being given any. But you didn't hear it from me.

The Flirt

As the Comedian and the Blabbermouth use jokes and smalltalk to mask missing screws in the engine room, the Flirt uses the oldest routine to avoid doing any actual work. Also recognizable early, the avoidance defense is sometimes more difficult to employ. If you're a compatible match, the Flirt is less easily swayed by early rejection, often mistaking "Go away" for coy encouragement. Sometimes mentioning your significant other will work, but the surest way to turn a cold shower on a hot flirt is the old Flip-Your-Preference routine. Whichever way the Flirt is playing you, make it clear you swing the other. By making yourself an unequal equation, the Flirt is deflowered and the dilemma defused.

The Complainer

This is the person who sits beside you and sees everything as bad from the weather to the world and will tell you so at every opportunity. Easy to spot because everything they say is negative. If you're alert you can I.D. them by their third or fourth sentence, and immediately banish them from your mind forever. With early detection you can stomp them out before they begin raging like an out-of-control negative wildfire of spewing hatred. They live by sucking up the air we breathe. You have to suffocate them with silence or you might accidentally inhale their negative molecules and take them home with you and get negative energy all over your house, and you know how hard that is to get rid of. Pretend you're busy, or deaf, or French, but whatever you have to do, don't say a word in their direction or you'll just be fanning the flames of nasty.

The Sweating Nervous Wreck

Dangerous because they're petrified to do anything. Whatever they touch breaks because they know it going in and prove the theory of self-fulfilling prophesies. If you help them early, you run the risk of adopting a wreck for life. Although if you don't they may have every piece of equipment broken before anyone—including you—has a chance to use it. Best advice: Give them every simple mindless task you can, like typing envelopes or sorting papers, while you do the real work. Set them up at a remote location to do the job. Perhaps Peru.

Obviously the bulk of the people you work with will not be one of these potholes on the highway of life, but spotting them early and steering clear of their pitfalls will make temping a more profitable and pleasant experience. Happy surfing, and don't slip on the Flipper.

Winning Points on Bad Days

The key in lousy situations isn't just surviving the day—which you've probably done before unless you were born yesterday—the trick is to actually win points in the opposing building. Here's how:

If by an unfortunate clerical error you've entered the Nightmare Job From Hell Zone and you know it, clap your hands. No I mean, call your agent. The agencies need to know what the situation is on the jobfront because they're just the dispatchers of bad news—you're the one who drives through the minefields. Temps are the only people who can give the home office any real feedback and they rely on the accuracy of your reports.

If you're calling in with bad news, don't whine, don't threaten to walk off the job, but once again use the PHAST approach. Call your counselor and say, "Hey Sandy, this place is just *covered* in gray carpeting," and then proceed to be very straightforward about what the problem is. They appreciate this. Plus it sets you up for a gold typewriter ribbon if you prove that even under these now-reported adverse conditions you did the professional thing and stayed on the job.

Counselors value temps who can call in honest, accurate and fast reports. Far too often, when temps find themselves on bad assignments they pull one of the Three Bonehead Moves:

1. The temp calls and complains about the rate not being high enough or the weather not being nice enough or the bus not coming fast enough or whatever twisted unimportant factoids clog the brains of the half-wits of the universe.
2. The temp leaves the job in the middle of the day.
3. The temp blows up at the client and insults them.

Since one of these scenarios is playing out at some agency right at this exact moment, by avoiding the 3 BM's you increase longevity at your agency by over 200 percent!

Never ever *ever* walk off a job earlier than the earliest end time anyone quoted you (sometimes different times may be used and you're only bound to the soonest time you agreed to). If you walk out in the middle of the day you can pretty much kiss that agency goodbye, or at least you'll be permanently barred from its A-Team.

No matter how bad a job is, use the earlier Coping Strategies, including the PHAST track, with whoever's bothering you, take a long lunch, review the Chilling-Out Rules in chapter 3, get away in your head, and know that after 5:00 this will never happen again.

But what if it just gets worse? What if you know it's the Job From Hell and you've only been there an hour? And worse, you've accepted it as a prebooked assignment for a week! Best advice: Call your agent, explain the situation PHAST. Tell them you realize you're booked for the week but would appreciate being pulled as soon as possible. A good agent knows what you're saying and will begin looking for a replacement for you, if possible; they're paid to know that if you're not happy you won't perform well and it doesn't do the client, the temp, or the agency any good to prolong a bad situation. Bad agents will demand you finish the week.

It's a good idea to hold off on your distress call until after lunch to see if there's any chance it may turn out okay. Many jobs that look unbearable in the morning will turn around by the afternoon. If you employ the various coping mechanisms outlined in this book, you may be able to turn the bad situation to your advantage by proving yourself and standing firm. Once you make the phone call and ask to be replaced, you've committed yourself to quitting.

After you develop a rapport with your agent, you may be able to call and give her a yellow light warning signal so she's alerted to the possibility of trouble but doesn't begin to take action. By honestly informing her of the problem you win points for being up-front. If you survive the day and agree to return, agencies will see you're an all-star who won't walk away from a tough assignment, and you'll earn another gold typewriter ribbon on your side of the balance sheet of life.

For another alternative to Life in the Hell Zone, see "Battle Pay" in the next chapter. Getting more money for doing the same work is what made this country great.

Let's Review

Take the PHAST track when you run into trouble; carry an emotional umbrella at all times for the days it seems to be raining wherever you go; learn to recognize dangerous coworkers and take preemptive strikes; stay on the job until it's done; when in trouble ask what troubles the troublemaker; you can't always control what's happening around you but you can always control your reaction to it.

10

-Advanced Functions-
Supporting the Arts

Okay, after that ample coverage of when things are rotten, let's get into the essence of temping, namely:

Downtime

There may be many reasons for becoming a temp, but what makes it the greatest profession on earth is that you're being graciously overpaid to sit at a top-of-the-line computer and $5,000 laser printer, with somebody else making the coffee and paying for the lights and with all the conveniences of modern life except maybe a remote control.

Apparently some people actually *prefer* doing other people's work and try to avoid downtime. Some search for downtime and rarely find it. Others have downtime thrust upon them. Whichever direction it blows for you, downtime is part of temping and you better be able to handle it as well as any other secretarial challenge or you'll never survive in the wild.

Look at it this way: Downtime is what you'd be doing if you were home anyway. You can read a book, write a book, pay your bills, avoid your bills, write your resumé and rewrite your future—

all with the added bonus of being paid for your time!

Or if you're not into books or bills, downtime can be your spiritual meditation time. Without the sin of distractions, you're confined to a chair with only the virtues of the mind. As with any meditation, no matter how much your mind may wander, it'll always come back to you, alone, where you are. There's no getting away from it. Downtime forces you to face your life. It's solitary confinement with supplies. It's time to figure out what you're here to do, and time to get started.

Downtime is the key to your future; if you can use it effectively, the rest of your life will be a breeze. It's like a daily Zen test: The longer you have downtime, the more enlightened you get. It's life enhancing. It's soul exciting. It's brain-booming magic!

A Little More Enlightenment, Please

Before each job, pack in your sidebag the Letterhead Tip Sheet, or *Mission Impossible* Dossier Folder, depending on how often you've worked there, then be sure to pack enough personal work to keep you busy for eight hours.

Fair Question: *"Eight hours of downtime?* Why did I read about all that work stuff? I already *know* how to sit in a chair."

Good Answer: You must learn how to work before you learn how not to.

One mistake you want to watch out for: When you go into a job trying to win them over, don't zip around all morning doing all the work there is to do totally A-Team perfect in two hours flat, only to inadvertently establish that as your standard performance level and get handed four days' work to do in one for the rest of your life. Ugh. Who wants that?!

Downtime Lesson Number One

Don't give them everything you've got in the first few hours or the rest of the staff will take the afternoon off and leave you the work to do.

The entire essence of doing your own stuff is this: You

must look like you're busy working. As long as you look busy when the Vice President of Greasy Hair walks by and you're just rippin' away on the keyboard and out of your third eye you see him watching you as he's thinking, "We must keep that temp." Meanwhile you're on page twelve of a letter to your mother. And tell me, what mother wouldn't appreciate that?

Without further digression we'll leap fingertips-first into the greatest software invention since the spell-check.

Opening Windows and Switching Screens

WordPerfect's switch-screen feature and Windows technology did for documents what the Mormons did for marriage: now you can have more than one going at once.

Here's how it works:

◆ Windows and multiple programs: By using Windows, not only can you be in multiple documents at once, you can work in different *programs* at the same time (as in, doing a spreadsheet for the boss in Excel while simultaneously writing your novel in Word). To have more than one program running, hold down the Alt and Tab keys together to switch between the applications one at a time; or click on the box with the minus sign in the upper left-hand corner above the File menu, then click on "Switch To..." This opens up the "Task List" box which lists all the programs you currently have open, plus the Program Manager, which allows you to open any other programs on the hard drive. Highlight the icon you want, double-click to open. Now you have more than one program running. Holding down Alt and hitting Tab you'll see a list of each program you have open, each indicated by a different screen. When you release the keys, the program shown will appear on the screen.

◆ WordPerfect: In version 5.1 or lower, hold down the shift

key and hit F3 to switch screens so you can have two documents open at once. Repeat the shift-F3 keystroke to switch back and forth between the two documents. In WordPerfect 6.0 for Windows and higher, click on the File menu option, then on New (or simply hit enter), then on Select (or enter). This opens a second blank document (or window) for you to work in. If you click on File again, then on Open, you can access files on a diskette in the a: drive. To see a list of all the documents you have open at any point, click on the Windows menu option and a list will automatically drop down naming each open file. If you need to save your document as a different version of WordPerfect, or even as another program, after you've worked on your document, click on File again, then choose the "Save As..." option. You'll see at the bottom of the screen the option to "Save File as Type." By clicking on the down arrow beside it, you'll see all versions of WordPerfect as options, plus other programs as well. Select one, and save as you normally would.

◆ Word for Windows: To open more than one document at once, click on the File menu option, then click on Open. Fortunately for the free world, uniformity has struck the world of word processing programs and document manipulation in most Windows word processing applications is pretty much the same. Happy switching!

With the caveat that you must actually be producing some work during the day, using screen-switching allows you to have a half-typed business letter open on one screen while you do your own work on the other. Most of the word processing secretaries in the world already know about this, and just about none of their bosses, so we all keep it quiet. Switching screens has been the greatest single contributor to the arts since the invention of the ticket booth, and the CEOs and their Republican puppets who are trying to destroy the National Endowment for the Arts are unwittingly funding an entire generation of pornographic mutant nympho turtles right under their stuffy noses.

Remember, and frequently cite, our universal motto:

"Support the arts—hire a temp!"

Act Yourself: Scene One: Your desk and bay are covered with papers, there are a few things to do, but they aren't urgent—nothing you couldn't whip out in half-an-hour. Take one of the little word processing jobs and put it up on the typing stand and begin to type the first few words. This is your camouflage. It's vital you don't type very far into it if it's the only document you've got to work on because this is your excuse for being busy for the rest of the day. If you finish it you may be expected to do something else, but if anyone wanders by until you do, they'll see you're clearly in the middle of something and leave you alone. Meanwhile, you have whatever else you want to work on from your diary to your trilogy running on the other screen. Just like in any wild jungle, your survival depends on hearing the sounds of approaching danger and the speed of your switch-screen draw.

As long as The Man *thinks* you're working it doesn't really matter if any work actually gets done, except in terms of whether you want to come back there again. If you do, you have to at least leave a clean trail and not stacks of undone work.

Downtime Lesson Number Two
You're supposed to do the work that's left for you on your desk, so make sure you're completing the last of it just as the quitting bell rings.

Here's one of my favorite routines: You're at your desk, there's some minuscule amount of work that you've propped up on the typing stand like a big green camouflage mountain, then you set to work on your diary, letter, or Great American Resumé until such time as you've got your papers and notes scattered all over the desk and you're holding seventeen thoughts at once connecting one note to another in a concentrated flurry of productivity. Just then you look up and there's some suit who works for the Man standing over you, papers in hand, and you think, "Oh-oh," but he says, "Oh no, I can see you're swamped. I'll have someone else do this. Sorry to disturb you."

All you need to collect is seven or eight of these and you're pretty much guaranteed induction into the Radar O'Reilly Hall of Temporary Fame.

Solving SoftSolutions

Many companies have started to catch on to us. In order to thwart the use of personal documents at work they've installed document management programs such as SoftSolutions or P.C. Docs. These act as a central storage and filing system that requires all documents to be saved on the network mainframe and given coded numbers that identify who created it, who edited it, and when.

If you create a document from scratch at work, the easiest way to take it home with you on a diskette is to perform your program's equivalent to the following:

Select/block the entire document.

Append or move it to A:filename.

You can always do a block move to A: anytime, as long as you give it a filename in the append or move command. You have now stored your document on your A: drive diskette for easy transport.

If you want to work on a longer document that you brought in on a diskette from home, it's a little more complicated.

1. Exit whatever document you're in to get back to the main SoftSolutions Options menu.
2. While in the Options menu, press 1 to get the Utilities menu.
3. While in the Utilities menu, press N for "Import Non-Profiled Documents."
4. You'll now get a screen that asks you to "Load-Path." Insert your diskette in the floppy drive, type "A:" then enter.
5. It asks you for the "File Template." You must know the

name of, and type in, the specific filename you want to work on. Hit enter when done.

Note: You have now actually *moved* the document from your A: drive diskette. *You no longer have the document on your diskette*. This was *not* a *copy* function.

6. You'll then be asked to confirm the creation of a new profile. You must hit "y" for yes because that's the whole point of these SoftSolutions-type storage programs—to have all documents "profiled" (and probably before long they'll be fingerprinting the keyboard input, but we'll figure out a way around that one, too!) A profile is like a computerized index card that requires certain fields of information to be filled in so the document may be found and cross-referenced many different ways.

7. Once you're in the document profile screen, under Document Name call it something like "delete later" or "scrap notes" so that anyone looking at the document in the future will know to delete it.

8. Fill out all the other Author and Document Type fields the way you normally would.

9. The document is now on the system and you can press Open to begin working on it, resaving it during the day as needed.

10. When you're ready to put it back on your diskette, return to the SoftSolutions main Options menu.

11. Select the "Check Out" option in order to move the document to the A: drive, and use these answers to their questions:

Copy out document	Yes	Path: **A:**
Copy of profile	No	Filename: **new name**
Check out document	Yes (is de-faulted)	

Under Filename I suggest saving to a *new* name to distinguish the document you created today from any other versions until you've tested this tweezers and gum combo on your own system and know it works.

12. Note the document is being both "copied" and "checked out." Once the profiled document is checked out, the main Options menu switches from the Check Out command you just used to Check *In* because the program knows that's the next step for this particular numbered document since it's not in the system anymore. When you select this Check In option it checks the document back in, *but also leaves the copy on your A: drive diskette.*

The reason you want to check it back in is because you don't want to leave documents in a "checked out" status, or "gone," under your log-in name and hours of employment. Remember your Temp Commandment: Leave no trail.

13. Now that you've got the document safely backed up on your diskette, you need to destroy it on the main system unless you don't mind Big Brother and The Whole Ding Company reading your secret scatological doodlings.

Some versions have Delete File on the main Option menu, which makes things easy, but if they don't, use the profile number to open up the document again. Block all the text in the document, then hit delete. It will ask, "Are you sure?" Answer "y" for yes. Now resave the document with absolutely nothing in it, stored under the original filename I suggested, such as "delete me."

14. Before you exit and leave, be sure to double-check that there aren't old versions of your document(s) stored in memory. To do this, select Versions from the main Options menu. A sub-menu comes up and you can select Delete to delete all old versions. Old versions can always be deleted, only the newest current version is protected and sometimes requires the internal block and delete method.

And that's the detour around that digital pothole.

The Bizarre Brotherhood of the Temps

As David Amram told us in the beginning, we have to pull together and share what we've learned with each other.

A good way to do this is to network with the other temps you meet on the beat. Quite frequently two or more of us will be stationed on the same assignment, which can be quite fun. Temps can come in any combination of funny, flamboyant, flaky, or phoney. It can be quite a show whenever two or more of us are in the same conference room together because if you're a temp you can't help collecting thousands of stories and sometimes we like to out-adventure the other. Everybody uses their temp money and freedom to do different things like traveling to exotic islands or financing a rock group, which seems to be the choice of choices among young temps these days. Temps are proud individualistic birds, the pluming dandies of their own private fantasies, and when you release five of them in the same pen together it's fun to watch them strut around brushing tales and relishing embellishments.

There's a certain road ethic and knowing nod among temps who've been doing it for years. If Adventure Cards count for anything in that Great Casino in the Sky, we're all holding royal flushes. More temps have done more interesting things than any ten lunchrooms of full-time workers. In fact, you'll start meeting and talking to more and more temps the more you work and after a hundred cool ones have slipped through your typing fingers you'll begin speaking up and networking with those who are in both your financial and creative profession. All temps do many things. Many things are behind doors. All doors can open. Step forward and push.

One of the more lucrative opening lines to a fellow temp is: "What agency do you work for?" Even if it's the same one as yours, ask about others. Every temp gets money for recommending another to their agency.

Trade tips. Ask if he's got an extra timesheet, then write his name on the perforated end to remind you. Now you've got the timesheet as a physical inducement to call the agency with your now well-rehearsed round of reconnaissance questions.

By using only agencies that working temps are using, you know they are busy and solvent. It's the other temps out in the field who are the most attuned to the traffic flows of the business. Gain from them when you're among them. Share knowledge. It's the best thing we've got.

Besides offering leads to new agencies, most temps are in the arts or are otherwise interesting people. They may be in your line of passion-bliss or may be able to share a story that relates to you because temps are all on roughly the same semipro level of development and still pursuing the dream full-bore, so they know how to find a rent-a-truck on a Sunday, or which clubs are ripping people off, or how to get health insurance, which by the end of the book you'll know all about, too. The insurance, not the truck. That was *The Truck Survival Guide* which was next to this on the shelf. You've picked up the wrong book. Sorry.

Battle Pay

Another interesting option to increase your bottom line is to cut right to it.

Agents know full well that certain seats at certain companies are hell-jobs where some inhuman boss-type person bites the heads off his help. Unfortunately for the rest of us, these people exist. And someone's got to sit outside their offices. After they've killed off many a young temp and Pickett's Agency has no more foot soldiers to send into the blazing fire, occasionally the agencies will turn to one of their superstars to try and hold on to the account and get through one more day.

When you reach superstar status and get a call like this and your counselor says something like, "It's a tough spot," that's your cue to ask, "How tough?" After they're done answering, you say, "It sounds like a really rough proposition and I don't want to put myself through the grief, but if you want to pay me my evening [or graveyard] rate for the day job, I might be able to see it through for a day."

The job they're asking you to do is worse and more difficult than what is usually asked of you, so logically you should be paid more since you're doing more. This should be attempted only if you've perfected the Umbrella Method from the previous chapter and are able to let insults and horrible people roll off you like raindrops from an umbrella. If you can perform the old Tune-'Em-Out-and-Just-Keep-Typin' routine, then ask for the higher rate and be compensated for your skill.

Raises

Once you've been on the A-Team for a while, you should have received a pay raise. Have you been consistently reliable for them? Collected several gold typewriter ribbons? Been flexible and amiable? Been nimble and been quick? Improved your skills, learned more functions, more programs, more corporate styles?

Ask other temps about their rates. Share knowledge, but don't tell your agency you're discussing rates with other temps. They hate this more than a little bit. One reason a temp may get a low rate is that she doesn't ask for a higher one. But remember: if an agency finds out you asked another temp her rate or told her yours, both of you risk being ostracized by the agency, and it'll cost you both money. So we never discuss our rates with each other, do we?

If your current agency won't pay you the highest rate available in your town but is treating you like an all-star A-Team player—which means using you all the time and in tough assignments—then you can rightfully demand a raise or start working at another agency. If you feel you deserve it, a good way to assess your value is to call new agencies and tell them what you want. This is the same kind of reconnaissance call you made way back in the beginning except it's rate-specific. This time, knowing the amount you think you're worth, you say, "I'm an excellent word processor and have been working at $X per hour and want to know if you get much work to support that rate." If they say yes, either go in there immediately, or tell your first agency this development and see if they're willing to match it or lose you.

No two cities are priced the same. Each city works out its own rate structure and some skills are inexplicably higher or lower than the next closest town. Check your local city. Your skills will have a basic pay rate and all agencies in each community are going to know what it is. There will be a range of a dollar one way or the other that you'll be in at any given time—until you climb a whole new skill level or master a new area of specialty. That's why your agency should volunteer to pay you the higher dollar of the two as soon as you've earned it because they know you'd get it elsewhere anyway.

For furthering your fortunes even further, there's a school of thought whose motto goes, "If you learn one word processing program, you've learned them all." It's the same old functions, only a different key. Ask your counselor which programs are paying the most and learn them and make the most money and drop me a line sometime.

Getting Canceled but Getting Paid

A fact of life in our Temporary World is that some companies consider temps somewhere below newts on the food chain. They will, for instance, book you in advance for the morning of January 1st, July 5th, or December 26th because there's a one in a thousand chance they may want to do some work and they don't want to inconvenience themselves or their employees so they go ahead and book you. Then when they come to that morning and realize they couldn't go into the kitchen let alone work, they call and cancel you at 8 or 9 A.M. after you've suspended your holiday fun or vacation plans in order to work for them.

All agencies have set policies for cancellations. The professional agencies that I recommend you work for should have a twenty-four hours advance policy, which means if you haven't been cancelled twenty-four hours prior to the start of the job assignment you're guaranteed at least a half-day's pay. This policy deters the kinds of booking and canceling abuse that some companies like to practice.

It's essential you know your agency's cancellation policy before you become a victim of it. It's up to you to ask your counselor in advance, so you both know the rules. Ethical companies and ethical agencies will not cancel arbitrarily or regularly. Not only are cancellations unfair and inconvenient, they jeopardize your making a living. If it's Monday and an agency books you for Thursday and you accept, you are now shut out of taking a week-long assignment elsewhere. Then when they cancel Wednesday night or Thursday morning, you lost a week's pay for nothing.

So you want to hit them in their pocketbook while fattening yours at the same time. Here's how:

Knowing your agency's policy is the required first step. The good ones will make the client pay for the booking. Others will bend over backward and kiss their own ass in a crowd to make the client happy and allow cancellations any time. If these agencies catch you at home before you leave the house for work—including the same hour as the job was scheduled—they can cancel the assignment and you have no fiscal recourse. Here's the trick:

Even agencies that won't pay temps' cancellation fees will usually pay a four-hour minimum or two hours for travel time if you couldn't be reached with the news of the cancellation and actually show up at the jobsite on time. Translation: if you're with one of these cheapo agencies and you fear cancellation but are revved up to go in, even if just for that four-hour minimum, be unreachable prior to the start of the job. Screen your phone calls. Leave early to run some errands before work. If it's a day shift, it's perfectly understandable that you slept at a friend's the night before. That way, you arrive at work at the appointed time, not knowing about the blinking red light on your answering machine. Once you're there, exactly as you were booked to be, a minimum payment is usually in order.

As we've discussed, unfortunately some clients and some agencies will try to take advantage of you, given the chance. They don't see that it's wrong for them to expect you to give up your day or week to be on call for them for no pay—which you're perfectly free to fall victim to. Or you can "not be available" to hear the cancellation call the hour before showtime and arrive on the dot of your appointed assignment, distinguishing yourself as a professional, and getting paid for your services.

The Royal Review

"Down Time, down boy. Here, go get your ball." Milk thee golden bovine of thyme; your chair is your home and you can meditate your way to a whole new life; use Windows or switch-screen to write your book, but always produce the work asked of you; talk to other temps about their agencies and where else they work and what else they do beyond this and if they're cute ask them to go to a good show you were planning to see anyway.

11

-Blizzards, Flu Season, and Other Highlights of Temping-

Blizzards, train strikes, and flu season are your new best friends! Anything that keeps other workers away from their appointed rounds is a time for you to earn a month's salary in a couple of twenty-four-hour shifts. Once you get into places of employment during a manpower shortage, they'll usually allow you to stay as long as you want to keep working.

You know the phrase, "The flu bug's going around." Why do you know it? Because all of a sudden at one time a whole bunch of people get sick. And what happens when people get sick? *They stay home.* And what do you do? Cash in like the rose man on Valentine's Day.

How about the news report: "If you don't have to drive—don't. The roads are a mess." This is a great time to immediately leave the house—because no one else does. When you hear this kind of good news on the radio, call your agencies and let them know you're a road warrior who cannot be stopped.

Timing your availability correctly is one of the best areas in which to distinguish yourself from the pack. Everyone can type, answer phones and say hello, but they don't all know when to call to get the jobs. Knowing the best times during the day cycle (chapter 6) is as important as knowing the best times during the year cycle (this chapter).

Summertime Blues

Job opportunities also arise during nice weather, of course. On sunny summer weekends, agencies will ring you silly. Taking those assignments is a small risk for a big payoff: About 25 percent of the time you end up working nonstop for some peon who has to get something done and is steaming mad because all his friends are out on a boat with his current fantasy-obsession dream-date but he's forced to be here in this crummy office *with you*—and by God you're going to pay for it.

The other 75 percent of those beautiful summer afternoon assignments, the person who called you will be sitting there looking out the window, then down at the page in front of him to make a little mark, then look out the window again, then he starts absently tapping the desk with the eraser end of his pencil slowly at first then a little faster until all of a sudden he throws it down so it shoots like a torpedo across the desk until it hits a book. He abruptly stands up, his chair rolling back into the credenza, and he marches out all determined toward you, handing you the draft he's made the one tiny mark on, and saying, "Here. Make these changes. While you're doing that I'm just going to step out for a minute," and he leaves until it gets dark. Can you sing, "Happy Days Are Here Again"?

And we mustn't forget the very orthodox Out-of-Town religion, practiced by millions of Americans. Comprised equally of secretaries and executives, Out-of-Towner's Holy Days are every weekend between May and September. This very large but largely ignored segment of our population abandons the offices of our cities before sundown on Friday, leaving a guaranteed bankable hole in the workforce for you to get in the habit of filling.

Can I also point out here that while these devout Out-of-Towners are idling in their cars on their pilgrimage to tourist attractions far and wide, you're collecting their double-coin and company dinners in an empty city. When they return home, reopening the backroads to the real wildlife, you're free to go midweek to their vacated vacation spots.

Moving in on Mondays

The trick is not only spotting trends, but milking them for all the cash they're worth. For instance, what day are most jobs in the temp industry filled? (Hint: "I Don't Like ____days")

Moving in on Mondays is one of the central sources of success in temping. Most of the temp jobs in America are filled between the hours of 7:30 and 10:30 A.M. on Monday morning. All you have to do to play that lottery is be awake and phone your counselor.

On Fridays, companies fire people, and 2-week notices come to an end. On Mondays people quit, call in sick, actually are sick, prolong vacations and prolong weekends, new projects are launched, new people are needed, new quarters begin, new expansions unfurl, new clients arrive, new competition appears, new deadlines emerge, new paperwork is added until the stack gets too high and "Enough is enough—let's call in a temp" is heard across the land!

It's also the day your new adventure begins! Knowing this, over the weekend you can plan to be dispatched. Since you're going to be well paid for the week and you know you're going to get sent out during those high-percentage Monday morning hours, it's worth your time to prepare on Sundays like a fireman ready to fly out the door at the first word of a call. By preparing your clothes, personal effects, and downtime projects in advance, you'll sound more prepared over the phone to your counselor, you'll get out the door faster when the call comes, you'll be early or on time instead of the procrastinator's alternative, and you'll get more out of your day financially and otherwise.

Monday is when assignments are booked for the whole week. Most of these will be announced to you as "It's for today, and may get extended for the week." And that really means "They're trying you out and they have their eye on you." If you do well and spread their mustard, you'll be there for the week or more. If they don't like you, it's a one-day assignment; they'll sign your timesheet and say goodbye.

Sacrificing Seinfeld to Survive

If you want a "here's how" that'll pay for itself a hundred times over, make sure you're fairly sober and can stand upright without much assistance by 4 P.M. any Thursday afternoon, then call your agency with your availability, "ready now." You'll be working within an hour.

Just as most new projects start on Mondays, most are due on Fridays. One of the essential truths we all learned in school was that nobody hands in their projects on time except those same few goody two-shoes in the front row. If it was up to them, temps would never get any work. Fortunately for the world's economy (or at least ours), most people dillydally around until the night before anything's due and then call in a fleet of temps to help them. Unfortunately, this means many of us miss *Friends* and *Seinfeld* on Thursday nights, but it's a small price to help nail them goody-goods.

Fridays in December

Or how about this one—this one's worth a million dollars. In fact I was going to save it for the sequel starring Sylvester Stallone but okay—just don't tell anyone else though, eh? Here it is: Fridays, in December, between 4 and 4:30 P.M. Here's why:

Everybody's in a great mood in December and jobs are flowing like beer at a hockey game. By sneaking in the door just as it's closing on the workweek, you're getting in with the people who are working late, and who are probably counting on a big bonus which they haven't yet been disappointed by not getting so they're going to be working all weekend long. By cracking that Friday night nut, and being really nice and helpful and careful to order everyone an extremely large dinner with secret desserts for later, they're going to be damn sure to ask you to return to work with them all weekend, which is exactly when you collect the highest rates, do the least work, and wear the coolest clothes.

During the November–December stretch you can branch out.

Tell your counselor as early as November 1 that you're willing to do any oddball work she might get in. No matter what skills you have, there are jobs from decorating banquette halls to blowing up balloons to being errand boys or grocery shoppers. Again, it's your flexibility when the job orders are coming in too fast to fill that the agency will remember later when times are slow.

Talk to the full-time employees when you're temping at one of your regular places, which you should now have a Secret Dossier Folder on, and study the company's particular weekly and monthly work patterns. Remember the Temp Commandment:

"Work does not come to you: You must go to it."

But then I always preferred the original acoustic version:

"Work does not come to you, and you do not do any of it."

The sooner you see and adapt to the patterns in your own employment community—whatever field you're in—the sooner you'll be coming in on the downbeat and cashing in on the jam.

Celebrate Holy America!

Fortunately, after two hundred years of letting everybody and their God in the door, we have more holy holidays than there are days in the year. As a Temporary Pagan, every day's a holiday and you never have to be anywhere. Personally, that's why I converted. That, and the really big collection plate and the fact that you get to be your own God.

Besides the obvious symbiotic opportunities for Jews working on Easter and Christmas, and Christians working over Passover and Hanukkah, as a trend-surfing money-hungry temp, don't forget the neediest and the less-well-known sects such as the Baseballites with their annual October rites. Millions of otherwise normal-looking Americans stay away from their jobs for nearly a fortnight as they gather round the preachers and pitchers for their sermons on the mounds, piously celebrating the ancient verities of win-at-all-costs, keep the home-field advantage, and get a piece of the concessions.

These and other less-ridiculous trends provide observant temps with the opportunities to earn several days of work before their less canny temp colleagues even know there's an opening. Zzzzzip-lock!

"My Theory" by A. Temp

Certain Ph.Ds try to make the following theory more complicated than it really is or stretch it out in order to base an entire miniseries on it when all I can really do is hum this old Monty Python tune:

The theory that I have follows the lines that I'm about to relate: The next thing that I am about to write will be my theory: This is how it goes: *All years are thin at one end, a little bit thicker in the middle, and much, much thicker at the far end.* That is my theory.

By far the slowest month of the year is January, and, amazingly, the second slowest is February! March is only a little better, then things start to open up by April and May. June, July, and August are green-surfing months as everyone goes on vacation, then September's really busy because students drop out of the temp market and return to their keg parties. October is always busy—I don't know why but it is, although I have my eye on the Baseballites. November is always really busy because every business is preparing their last full push before the Thanksgiving recess. All of December is insane and you could work twenty-four hours a day for thirty-one days if you wanted to, which I recommend because by January first the party's over and you have all those resolutions to deal with.

I hope it's extremely clear that the direction of the line in this graph goes steadily upward from the slowest month of January to the busiest month of December as the temp industry experiences one healthy climb up, up and away, until its abrupt drop-off in January and we begin the new year's cycle. So of course the hardest part is →

Surviving the January–February Freeze-Out

It's during this two-month freeze-out that regular workers realize they spent too much money over the holidays and they can't afford to take a single day off. Businesses are slow because nobody's spending money so there's just this national—and more importantly, local—deep freeze. You need to make the decision to hibernate, or else really be on your toes and play the game right to get steady work during January and February.

The rest of this chapter is devoted to surviving and thriving during this downturn.

First, before outlining a ton of tips, I want to make one little plea for frugality. This is the time of year for it, and this is the only time I'll ever mention it. All you have to do is sketch out the following simple chart of your expenditures.

The Ongoing Expense Report

Create a personal chart like the one in Example Eh? Many of the figures you will only know by the month, such as the rent, so plug that into the Per Month column, then multiply by twelve for the year column, divide by four to figure out the week, and by thirty to figure out how much rent you actually pay per day. Other figures you might only know per day, like a newspaper, so plug that into the Per Day column, and then multiply by seven for the week column and thirty for the month. Others, like your average transportation expenses are best calculated on a weekly basis, and things like annual dues for clubs or insurance go in the Per Year column first, then are divided down. This way, each and every one of your expenses is calculated per day, week, month, and year.

This is the most successful method I've seen at getting people to cut down on their real expenses and increase their real earnings. With each and every time frame covered, every cent you spend has a column. A couple six-packs of beer a week are almost $800 a year. $5 for lunch is over $1,000 per year. Your rent is actually $17 a day! Always round the numbers to their higher amount because it's better to budget high and have an extra nickel than to budget low and come up short.

The January–February slowdown is the time of year to review your own personal Ongoing Expense Report to see where you need to cut back. We all get fat over the holidays, and this is the most realistic and cost-effective diet there is.

You can make a new chart every year and put the old one in

your "Expenses" file so you can monitor how your spending habits change from year to year. But before I promise anything else, try it! Plug all the numbers you know into a chart along the following lines:

Example Eh?

The Ongoing Expense Report				
	Year	*Month*	*Week*	*Day*
Clothes	$200			
Birthday presents	100			
Dental plan	85			
Haircuts	80			
Rent		500		
Phone		50		
Electric/gas		40		
Groceries			25	
Entertainment			20	
Beer			15	
Laundry			5	
Lunch				5
Transportation				2.50
Newspaper				.50

Now that you have each of your expenses listed, and one number filled in beside it, multiply out the other columns.

The key is, in each category always start with that concrete finite number to multiply up or divide down to reach your other conclusions. Allow "Per Day" amounts to be exact, but round off all week, month, and year amounts to whole dollars. Use the following calculations to fill out your chart:

If you have the year: divide by 12 for the month
                        divide by 52 for the week
                        divide by 365 for the day

If you have the month:	multiply by 12 for the year
	divide by 4 for the week
	divide by 30 for the day
If you have the week:	multiply by 52 for the year
	multiply by 4 for the month
	divide by 7 for the day
If you have the day:	multiply by 365 for the year
	multiply by 30 for the month
	multiply by 7 for the week

Your new chart should have every column of every line filled in and look something like this:

Neat Eh?

The Ongoing Expense Report			
	Year	*Month*	*Week*	*Day*
Clothes	$ 200	17	4	.55
Birthday presents	100	8	2	.27
Dental plan	85	7	2	.23
Haircuts	80	7	2	.22
Rent	6,000	500	125	16.66
Phone	600	50	12	1.66
Electric/gas	480	40	10	1.33
Groceries	1,300	100	25	3.57
Entertainment	1,040	80	20	2.85
Beer	780	60	15	2.14
Laundry	260	20	5	.71
Lunch	1,825	150	35	5.00
Transportation	912	75	17	2.50
Newspaper	182	15	3	.50
Minimum:	$13,844	$ 1,129	$277	$38.19
	Per year	Per month	Per week	Per day

As you look at your chart, many new specific economic realizations should begin hitting you about now, such as you need to start making a whole lot more money right away!

Accountants' Disclaimer: If you take your month, week, and day totals and multiply them out to the yearly amount, you'll find that you get different totals, which is due to the rounding off of thirty days in a month etc. Always accept the highest number as the truth.

Now that you've constructed your basic budget, *refine your data.* If you're only buying lunch five days a week, don't multiply it by seven for the week. Then use the week as the finite number to calculate the month and year. This chart should be as precise as you can make it. It's for your eyes only. It's something you can work with in an ongoing way and you can modify the numbers as you modify your behavior. It's an honest approach and can be an open challenge to yourself to lower your most unpleasant numbers.

Frequent, Accurate, and Annotated Smart-Bomb Job Calls

During those first frigid weeks of January, begin talking to your agencies more frequently. Two times a day is not annoying, three is pushing it, and any more than that and you're asking for ostracism. Carefully pick your times of day and record all responses.

The best times to call are once between 8 and 9:30 A.M. and once between 4 and 5 P.M. for work that evening or the following day. By carefully selecting, monitoring, and adjusting your call-times to each agency, you're virtually guaranteed to make a "hit"— that is, be calling them right as a job is being called in by a client. Refer back to the "Timing" in chapter 6 if you need a refresher.

Indefinite Assignments and Lower Rates

Let your counselor know you're willing to take longer-term or "indefinite" assignments, and that you may consider a slightly lower rate if something interesting comes in. This signals to the agency that you're flexible. They like that. If you're a good temp they'll want to keep you on their roster and they know these slow months are times of change when people leave for long-term jobs or otherwise disappear. Being flexible during the time of year they need you to be will make them more likely to be flexible when you need them.

New Agencies

The New Year's lull is also the best time to explore new agencies using the same techniques outlined earlier. If you're interested in expanding your repertoire of agencies, this is a time when you're not under pressure and can begin to open up new possibilities to finance the rest of your year. I assume by now you've already got a few agencies under your belt, but unless you're overbooked every day of the year you can probably use one more card in your hand to draw from.

This quiet, unpressured slow season allows the new agency to send you out on an assignment and review your skills, as well as allowing you to assess the agency. Because most of the rest of the year is busy, you want to have your stable of agencies set up during the downtime so you can just run through a list of cozy counselors. You don't want to be taking full days out to apply at new agencies during the big-money months at the end of the year. Plus the agencies are so busy at that time they're more likely to rely on regulars who've proven themselves all year rather than take a chance on a new person who might screw up or not show up.

This is the slow time of the year after all, so be patient. You may interview but not get work with the new agency until March. Call, be cheery, stay in touch on a regular basis, show you're professional, and the agent will be happy to test you out on the job as soon as the opportunity arises. If you've made a good impression, the agent will be just as eager to see you working as you are.

Old Contacts

Once you've registered at an agency, as much as a year or more can go by without the two of you talking, but you can still call them up and say, "I registered with you last year. We haven't spoken in a while, but I just wanted to let you know I'm available." Once you get connected with your original counselor (assuming she still works there, which isn't always the case), tell her what you've been doing and what field(s) you're looking in. This is a very common and valid way to rekindle a business relationship. Your test scores will still be on record and if you did well and didn't get any N.G.s on assignments they sent you on, then you're a gift to them because you've gained another year's experience and you're a better player.

And tit for tat, just like that, agencies can call you up after years of silence. It always happens when things are insanely busy and you could probably open your own agency you've got so much work, and then *ring,* it's some place you haven't worked in two years wondering if you can go in to Citibank immediately. If you plant your seeds and tend to your garden, you can munch forever on the fruits of your labor.

Another idea beyond calling in to agencies is stopping in to agencies. It's the old "I was in the neighborhood and thought I'd stop by" routine. Since temp agencies are often clustered in the same neighborhood, you can probably "drop in" on all of your contacts in half an afternoon. Just say hi. Be up. Just stay high. Don't be down. Just drop by. You're no clown. Just say thanks. You're still around.

Also during this time, go back through your Letterhead Tip Sheet file, the single pages I suggested you gather from each assignment with the agency listed on each and the dates you worked there. Type up a quick list of all the places each agency sent you to over the past year or more that you want to return to. Your counselor's a) going to be impressed at your recall and b) will have forgotten about some of the places you mention and will be grateful for you reminding her of clients she hasn't phoned in a while.

Psst! As an added bonus—this always works.

Learning New Computer Programs

While you're on the phone running your valuable old contacts past your counselors and reestablishing that symbiotic bond, ask them which computer programs, besides the one(s) you know, are getting the most calls for work. Since it's going to be slow and you'll be too busy the rest of the year anyway, this is the season to learn new programs. By having an open dialogue with counselors at more than one agency you'll hear a variety of answers and can learn the most commonly cited program.

Different professions and regions of the country have different programs in use and in demand. A survey of your weekend Help Wanted pages will tell you what's happening in your market this month. Of course, the first thing to do is learn your primary program inside out, because once you're fluent in one language you'll realize how similar they all are.

Branching out and learning new programs is as important as learning your first one. Computers, like the world, change every day. No program is going to last. It's their nature to be upgraded and improved. Therefore, if you intend to make your living near a computer, you'll forever need to be open to learning as many new programs as possible. Accept and embrace that tenet and you'll be employed for the rest of your life. The more programs you know, the more money you'll have to spend on your loved ones.

And it's not just computer systems. It's everything! The world is no longer an assembly line and we're no longer rivets. There is no green pasture, no quick lotto ticket, no gold watch, but now you can watch the gold build up if you keep up with your skills. If you think the world changes rapidly now, flip ahead to tomorrow. No profession is going to last longer than a game of chance.

If there's one thing you get from this book, I hope it's the knowledge that to survive, let alone succeed at the turn of the millennium, you're going to need to be fast on your feet and able to constantly adapt to new environments. Nothing will be around for long (including our species if we keep this up), but if you want to survive, for God's sake don't limit yourself in your mind to only one way of making a living. The only permanent job you're ever going to have is daisy fertilizer. Since you'll be fairly stuck at that point, you may as well go on as many different rides as you can while you're still at the fair.

"Welcome to Computerworld at Worldworld, we hope you're enjoying your visit so far. I'm VoiceInsideYourHeadMan, and I'll be your host for this part of the show. First off, is there anybody here from out of town? Good, good. Okay, now we're going to show you how to learn new computer programs, and then a little later we'll show you how to milk the big fat cows. Anybody want to learn how to milk the big fat cows? Good, good. Now, how about if we learn new computer programs for free? Okay. Make sure the bar is securely fastened in front of you, and remember, no standing up while the ride's in progress. Have fun!"

Ways to Learn

On the job

With the advent of Windows technology, every computer you sit at has many different programs. The very best way to learn a new program is while you're being paid to be working on another. During the aforementioned downtime instead of writing the aforementioned Great American Whatever, another option is switching to the Program Manager (alt-tab) and calling up one of the other programs. All programs come with tutorials that allow you to learn at your own speed. Once your agent survey or Sunday Help Wanted section tells you which programs are the most in demand, go ahead and start with screen one of the tutorial, or else create a test document and begin manipulating the text.

155

Your agency

All employment agencies worth the timesheets they're printed on will have their own computers to both test and train temps. These computers are sitting there for the sole purpose of serving you. Use the January–February freeze-out to learn a new program. You can probably do it in one day, depending on your skill level. Also, you can use this as a variation on the stand-by routine that was outlined earlier. If you come in dressed to go on an assignment and a job order happens to come in that you could fill, you may have a bit of a jump on the other temp.

Get with the program

The best way to learn and be proficient at any program is to use it at home. Beg, buy, borrow, steal, but get the program. If your hard disk is too full to add more programs, be advised that gigabyte hard drives (that's a billion bytes if you're counting) are under $200 now (although by the time you read this they'll probably be about $20). Consult Computer Shopper *magazine and you'll find many different companies who will UPS one to you wrapped in enough foam to survive an air drop, and you can load that gigabyte with programs that will pay for it in a day. And as they say in the band, if you don't have a gig you're just playing with yourself.*

Getting Money Back on Your Taxes

If you temped last year, you should be getting money back on your income taxes—which is kind of a wild and wonderful concept all in itself! The reason is because agencies withhold your income tax based on the high rate you earn per hour. Since you won't be sustaining that high rate all year due to taking time off and not working 100 percent of the time, you'll have had your taxes withheld at a rate exceeding your final earnings. That extra money is the refund you will receive.

If this is the case for you as it is for most temps, get in the habit of filing your taxes early each year so you'll receive your check during these slow months when you need it. Mark your yearly calendar for next January to pick up your income tax forms early from the post office so you can file as soon as you receive the W-2 forms from your agencies.

To have even more money taken out and therefore receive an even larger refund, check out the "Financial Planning" chapter in the "Richie Cunningham School of Do-Rightness" section at the end of the book.

Following Your Dreams

Once you've survived the holiday and don't have to speak to another relative for six months, the new year is the best time of year to pursue your dreams. Utilize this tranquil seasonal downturn when income is at its lowest anyway to focus on your own personal Big Picture.

Imagine going on an all-expense-paid vacation in a place very much like your place, with all the comforts of your personal creative home space. The phone is off. It's just you and your mind together forever to visit all those places you always wanted to go. This is the Free Gift time of year, the hidden months that most people miss, the secret time when the rest of the penguins are in slow-motion anyway. For once you can just stay home in your own no-distraction private spa retreat of work-free brain-play and relax.

Everybody else is stumbling around and grumbling at this time of year anyway so you may as well change your life. Distractions are down. Outside support for your endeavors is up because everyone is thinking of doing something Really Really Big and will gladly pat your back instead of breaking their own.

"Follow your bliss," is quoted a lot these days, but maybe that's because it's so true. Joseph Campbell said it and he was right. The other half of it went like this: "Follow your bliss and doors will open where there were no doors before."

If you're having trouble finding bliss, follow your goosebumps instead. They're your little Spirit Receivers popping up to catch the coded messages from the Great Navigator. When you see them, like bread crumbs, follow their path. Whenever they appear, the chi is channeling and these are the travel genies pointing you in the direction of your happiness. The road to success is a bumpy one, and sometimes it takes a little goose to get you started.

Tackle the projects you always dreamed of during these quiet months—the paintings, poems, inventions, or novels that are flying around your belfry when you can't sleep at night. Doors will open where there were no doors before. January. February. Doors will open.

"I'm always doing what I can't do yet, in order to learn how to do it," Vincent van Gogh said.

Once you begin at the beginning of the year, and you work and you work on your baby or your book, you utilize the shutdown nature of nature and incubate your child. And only you have the one that's inside you.

"All great spirits encounter fierce opposition from mediocre minds," Albert Einstein said.

You may encounter resistance from your closest allies but that's only because you've done such a good job at hiding what you were meant to be doing, that even those around you can't see it at first. Be forgiving while you ignore them.

"Stick to it in spite of hell and other people," is how Katherine Anne Porter put it.

Train, love, work, dream.

"In most men there exists a poet who died young, whom the man survived," the French poet Sauté Beure said.

This is the one beautiful unavoidably true time of year to linger within yourself, to turn the ringer off, to not visit the mailbox, but live in your chair and dance on your rug and dust your instrument off and sing!

"One may have a blazing hearth in one's soul, and yet no one comes to sit by it," wrote van Gogh.

Fuel your fire. Burn your wood. Stoke your soul.

Life only happens once.

Let's Review

Temping funds the fun without selling out the dream; the January–February downtime is the best time of year to make your dreams come true; pare down your expenses and delve into your own projects during the slow snow season when you have the chance to establish a work ethic with a laser beam focus that can stay with you the whole year through and maybe a lifetime; apply at new agencies; accept slightly lower rates; stoke your soul; learn new computer programs; and turn the shortest, coldest deep-freeze month of the year into the most productive month of your life—because a month is a terrible thing to waste.

12

-Milking the Cows-

Okay, now that you're pretty much an ace at this temping thing, the last really fundamental step is how to go in for eight hours and leave after thirty. Or at least make a whole ton of money toot sweet.

Let's assume you like the place, the pace, and the people, and you don't have anything else to do tonight. Here's a way to make tons of money:

If you're in at a large company that has a personnel office, one of the best things you can do for that supervisor is not to cause her any problems or force her to do any extra work. Consequently, they want you to handle all the needs of the person or people you're assigned to. If you're in nine to five and they're already thinking about getting someone to work five to twelve for the same person, and you want to do it, you can save the personnel supervisor another unnecessary job call by easing gracefully into the position.

Catching the 5:25

Providing that the company allows for their staff to earn overtime wages, the supervisor has an obligation to offer her own staff the overtime first. But if the call doesn't come in until closing time, she's not going to have time to fill it and will consequently think you're doing her a enormous favor by staying. It's the old 5:25 "Mr.-Bovine-just-said-he-wants-someone-to-stay" call. The trick is getting Mr. Bovine to ask for overtime at exactly that time. Here's how:

If people are working late, usually the day has been really busy and you can tell the Big Moo ain't knocking off anywhere near 5:30. He's in his office on conference calls and seems embroiled in a big kerfuffle over something. He's doing this and doing that and barely remembered to eat lunch by 3 P.M. If you like the guy and he's nice to you while he's in the middle of his Great Kerfuffle Debate, then you may want to work with him into the evening.

Should you decide to accept this possibility, poke your head in his office around 5:24. Since you developed a good working relationship during the day, Mr. B. trusts you and immediately looks up as you mouth in a stage whisper, "Do you need coverage after 5:30?" And he nods an enthusiastic wide-eyed *Yes*. The guy has been too busy to think about anything, has no idea what time it is, and now he thinks you've just done him an enormous favor by looking out for him when other temps or his regular secretary might have just walked out at quittin' time.

Now you call the personnel supervisor at 5:25 and truthfully say, "Mr. Bovine just requested coverage for tonight. He didn't say for how long but it looks like he's going to go late."

The poor personnel person has probably got her coat on and is ready to walk out the door when you call. "I hate that Bovine bull," she says. "He never lets me know anything. Can you do it?"

"Let me see..." (pause dramatically as you check your imaginary appointment book), "Okay, yeah, I guess I could."

"Oh boy, thanks a lot! You really bailed me out, SuperTemp. I owe you one." K'ching! One gold typewriter ribbon, please.

The Art of the Meal

Now that you're booked for the long haul extra shift, you're definitely in store for a massive free meal and car ride home.

If you're working late and there's not going to be a designated break for everyone to go out for dinner, which, of course, there never is, it's accepted custom for the company to pay for dinner for those who are working through it.

Since you're going to be the person ordering it, take a look around for the menu file of places they order from. Since the boss is too busy to know what day it is, you'll be doing him a favor by looking into dinner, and doing yourself one by picking your favorite menu from the selection. Once you've found it, you can begin picking out two or twelve dishes that might be to your liking. Since you'll be phoning in the order, picking it up at the door, and laying it out wherever it's to be eaten, I guess you'd be the only person who'd really know what was ordered.

Once you've played in the Temp Leagues for a few seasons you may find yourself in an extended conference room series where there are food spreads of sirloin steaks and Cornish hens with paper junkies working on some big deal around the clock for weeks, and you're ordering new meals night after night, trying to think of something different every time, and meanwhile you're bringing home so many entrees you can't cram another one in your freezer. Like I say, temping is hard work, but somebody has to do it.

Playing the Clock

You've caught the 5:25, you've padded the menus, and now you're just playing the clock. The main thing to keep in mind is never to remind Mr. Moo-Moo of the time. You want him to stay busy and distracted in his office until the cows come home, so to speak.

If he takes a break and comes out, always use reassuring sentences that direct the focus back to him and his quandary, such as, "Everything's under control here. How are you doing?"

Don't ask if there's anything you can do for him; that just makes him think that he really doesn't have anything for you to do and you should go home.

I recommend, "I'll be right here if you need me." It's the same thing without posing it as a question. You do not want them to think. Thinking bulls are dangerous. Keep them calm and stupid. You never want them interfering with your writing flow or cash flow. Also, delay each step as long as you can without going over the edge. Call the restaurant you selected and ask how late you can order a delivery. In normal circumstances, I recommend dinner no later than 8:30 or 9:00 because after that you begin to run the risk of him saying, "You know, it's getting late, let's call it a night," because he's suddenly thinking of his own kitchen or whatever. You hate that. There's nothing worse than smelling the bacon but going home hungry.

That's why around 8:30 or so you want to poke your head in the door or just slip the menu in front of him, or ask, "Do you want to order something?" They appreciate your picking the menu because it's one less decision they have to make. You have nothing to lose by trying since it's understood he can veto the restaurant if he doesn't like your choice. Successful businesspeople want answers, not more questions. Questions they've got all day. To be a Radar O'Reilly SuperTemp, give only answers and ye shall be rewarded.

When you order at the outer edge of permissible dinner ordering time, it doesn't get there till 9:00 or 9:30. You put your seven extra meals in the fridge and lay out Mr. Bovine's trough so that he's not even starting to guzzle'n'slurp again until 9:30 or 10. His body's thinking it's still 6:00, so you've got maybe six more hours of free coupons in Cashland.

What may occur during dinner is idle chat time. This can last anywhere from thirty seconds as he's passing through to thirty minutes if you have a formal sit-down idle chat. Either way, it taps into one of the essential services we temps provide: We're an "out," a pressure-valve release from the tension and stress that's giving him heart disease. You're an outside ear, an impartial listener, a different subject than the one he's been fighting over all day.

I've made tens of thousands of dollars just because I can listen and make the overworked feel better, maybe laugh, and perhaps forget for a minute or two that they live their lives in hell. I've noticed a few people are under pressure these days (although not temps). You've probably felt it if you've ever had a full-time job.

Somebody's bugging you to work more hours, make more money, do more work, do it faster, faster, and now do things you don't know how to do.

As a temp, all you master is filling in time. There's no stress whatsoever. And Aretha frankly, you don't care whether the company collapses tomorrow. These poor guys have got opposing lawyers and greedy CEOs and foreign banks all pushing and pulling at different parts of their carcass. When you know none of that is happening to you, it makes it easy to be sympathetic during their episodes of panic.

Bear in mind you have to watch yourself and not take your support rap too far. I've seen some temps try to entertain the poor overworked schmo with a bad comic routine that would have been yanked on open mike night, and they're promptly sent home without dessert.

The Old Knowing-Nod-'n'-Smile Routine

For silence and uninterrupted downtime, remember the simple rule that police use when interrogating a suspect or watching one in the field: Criminals make a mistake, blow their cover, or confess during an extended pause. It's in the void of nothingness that the guilty snap, when the truth is yapping at the silence until, like in "The Tell-Tale Heart," it comes bursting forth. A centered, grounded, not-guilty person can easily endure silence and inactivity because there's no confession bobbing under the surface. Patience is the key.

In terms of either playing the clock or milking the cows, the one thing you don't want to do is stir up work unnecessarily. Do not break the silence if you can bear it. Don't volunteer anything. Don't jar them awake. If you can help it, don't even remind them you're there.

The most successful technique is the old Knowing-Nod-'n'-Smile routine. It goes a little something like this: You hear the person coming, and you look up into their face, slowly shifting your mood from the concentrated work you're doing to the beginnings of the expressed happiness of a smile. You want this to grow gradually so by the moment you make eye contact your face instantly blooms into a full smile. Then you finish off with a slight but deliberate all-knowing nod like you're sharing the same inside joke.

It's weird, but it's almost 100 percent effective. I don't want to be too Stanislavskian about it, but perhaps I should discuss the motivation behind it. You want your smile and follow-up nod to be saying, "Hey, isn't what we're doing silly? It doesn't mean a thing, but still we have to do it. There's so much more than this. I know— you might pretend to get upset about things when you're on the phone, but you're in control. You know it, and I know it. This is just a tiny part of the big picture and everything's totally under control."

Once you've got that gradual smile beginning to bloom on your face and you're holding him in a smile face-lock, let your eyes begin to narrow just a little bit and the smile begin to grow as you notice his reciprocal response—then Ka'boom—*now* hit him with the deliberate knowing nod.

Works like a charm. Even if the two of you were thinking completely different thoughts, he's now positive you know exactly what he's thinking and you're agreeing with him, and the two of you carry on this silent, knowing, nodding conversation until he walks around the corner and another $100 spits out of the cash machine. K'ching!

The Old Getting-Somebody-Else-to-Do-Your-Work Routine

One of my all-time favorite tricks, which I still pull off several times a year, is the old Getting-Somebody-Else-to-Do-Your-Work Routine. Here's how it works:

Let's say it's busy and one of the permanent people isn't feeling that well, so you say, "Gee, you look just awful. Do you feel sick? Why don't you just go home and we'll call in another temp?" They couldn't agree more and call your agency. You immediately stop working, leave everything for the new temp to do, and promptly resume working on your own project. You get the downtime, the new temp gets the extra money, the agency gets the new job order, the sick person gets to go home, and the boss gets the shaft!

Then after you've played this one a few times, you can work this variation into your act: "There's way more work here than one person can do. I mean, you can either leave some for tomorrow, or maybe if it's not too late we can still get someone in to help us."

Or, in a pinch: "You don't expect this done, *too*, right?"

The Moral of the Story Department: Always carry your agency's phone number with you. Every time you pass it along it gets you one more gold typewriter ribbon toward Radar's Hall of Fame, which is positioned somewhere between here and the end of the hall, lingering near a water cooler on the fringes of...The Twilight Zone.

Write Your Screenplay and Get Paid for It

The most important key to longevity in the midnight hours is staying awake, and the best way to stay awake is to be deeply absorbed in your own work. The MooHeads actually appreciate this because it indicates you're alive.

I've seen many a temp wither on the vine because they're left at a desk without water and with nothing to do, and they didn't bring any supplies with them. After three or four hours of doing absolutely nothing with their lives they start slumping forward until they suddenly snap and both fists come crashing down on the desk as they scream out a death cry to be given work or to be sent home! Poor things. If there are two of us on the same assignment doing nothing, which frequently happens on big projects in corporate America, my partner temp will sometimes be sent home early while I'm still sitting there smokin' away on something. The other guy gets dismissed early and I milk another eight hours for simply being awake and doing my own stuff. K'ching!

Some people have trouble believing that employers or supervisors don't mind you doing your own work, but many a time have I heard a Cowlick moo, "Oh, I'm glad you brought in something to do, because it's going to be slow for a while."

Bovines know one of the biggest problems on the quiet night

shifts is keeping the staff alert and awake. Given nothing to do, some temps will start talking on the phone, usually making traceable long-distance calls and generally being a distracting voice in an otherwise quiet work world. Since Bovines often get sleepers or talkers as temps, you can see why people who are working and alerting are the preferred temporary alternatives.

More Money for Nothing

In terms of further sucking on the teat of the Moomeister, at the point where she's getting ready to leave, ask her, "Do you know what time the others are coming in the morning and do you need someone to stay until they get here?"

This often results in the response, "That would be really great if you can do it. Make these photocopies and leave them on Mr. Orwell's desk. I think he'll be in around 7:30, so if you could be here until the regular shift comes in that would be really super." This way, the cash cow wanders off around 2 A.M., and you've now got *another five and a half hours at least* of the after-midnight highest rates when absolutely *nothing* will be going on except you making money for doing your own work! K'ching, K'ching, K'powie!!

Once You're There You're In

If you don't manage to work around the clock but only pull off a "midnight," the next best thing is lining up work for tomorrow. Usually the person staying late is of bosslike stature, or at least feels that way by that hour, and will in all likelihood tell you to come back tomorrow if you ask.

One of the surest laws of employment is: Once you're there, you're in.

If you get the go-ahead, return in the morning to the workstation location you were at that night and call the secretarial supervisor to tell her you're there.

This may come as a good surprise or a bad surprise to her. You could have just won major brownie points for following the boss's directions, saving her work, coming through, and taking charge. Or if it's a bad surprise and they already have someone booked for that spot, they may put that person somewhere else because you're there first and are the obvious preference of Mr. Bovine who just requested you last night. Worst case scenario is they sit you somewhere else for a few hours, then send you home with half-a-day's pay.

What's most likely to happen is you're going to solidify your relationship with the all-night Jersey, and by extension, with the company at large. When one Bovine vouches for you, it's like the whole herd mooed.

You want to make one-on-one connections with the powerful wherever you go. One or two days of really concentrating on what you're doing and you can earn yourself free passage for a year. If you wow 'em early, that first impression will last longer than a Midas muffler. There are always going to be some places you go only once because you didn't make a powerful enough first impression. But with careful cultivation you can establish a whole range of pastures where you can graze and screw up two-out-of-three times because you won the eye of some big bull on the first day and have milking rights for life.

First Impressions: Use 'em or lose 'em.

Leave No Trail

Which segues nicely into Last Impressions. That is, the way you leave the desk, computer, and work space. You must live by your Temp Commandments, especially this one: Leave no trail—paper or otherwise.

Remember: Never underestimate the power of a secretary. If the personnel supervisor asks the opinion of the regular secretaries who worked near you and those respected union soldiers don't file a good report on you, forget about a return engagement.

Leave no crumbs, no coffee cups, no food-filled garbage can, no lipstick on the phone, no gum on the chair, no work left undone (except for what you can get away with). Leave no long-distance phone record that will be checked within days and whose date puts you at that seat, in which case you can wave bye-bye to your $200 nights on that ranch for life.

Cattle Roundup

Temping is a great profession and I make a lot of fun about utilizing downtime and scamming a little more here and there, but ultimately each job is the way you eat, drink, and pay the rent on that nice place you live in. There's all sorts of fun you can have within its confines, but ultimately it's the way you make your living. And you have to live, especially with yourself. This is your gig. Play the right thing.

13

-Going Permanent-

So now after all the fun we've had, maybe some of you are ready to settle down and get a steady job and stop all this surfing around. I mean, people left Woodstock before it was over, so it's not without precedent.

As we discussed earlier, "Temping is the most lucrative and practical job-search program in the world," period. In fact, three-quarters of you are going to use it as a way to full-time work, according to a recent survey by the National Association of Temporary and Staffing Services.

One of the reasons you likely considered temping in the first place was because you had skills and talent but weren't riding the same straight-line railroad track everybody else seemed to be on. Yours seemed to curve a little and wind around a lake. Through temping you've proven that your difference is your strength. After your myriad working experiences, you've watched your inner strength (and savings account) grow. You've proven to yourself that you can do it. You've learned the invaluable skill of independent living, and you should be careful not to surrender it too cheaply.

Many temps make the mistake of leaving a permanent job in order to play the field, only to instantly get sucked into the first job they come across. Be sure a full-time job is what you really want. Make sure it's in the field you want. Make sure it'll allow you to foster the talent and skills that are "you." If you've learned how to ace the tests, win over the first day, get called back, and milk the cows...honey, you can do anything.

The Comfort Rating Factor

Before taking the Big Plunge into Permanent Seas, be sure to talk to other people about what you're planning. Testing your Comfort Rating Factor can be done by verbalizing your intentions to your closest friends. The C.R.F. will help you determine if this is something you really want to do or if it's only a good *idea* of something to do. Was it an uplifting, invigorating feeling to say you were ready to go permanent? Or did you get a lump in your throat and a quiver in your liver? The more you can comfortably articulate the move and specify what you're looking for, the more your brain begins to solve the details of the problem. Neither it nor you can go forward or fully function with doubt and hesitation lingering in the neurons.

Don't worry, you're not going to be forced into a permanent job tomorrow. By making the decision with no definitive date requiring action, the power always remains with you. When you commit to needing a job by a certain date, the power shifts to the person who has the job to offer. As long as you're only considering relinquishing your freedom, you're a gift to them. Don't give yourself away cheap. They need your labor more than you need their company.

Pulling the C.R.F. chit-chat with loved ones also forces you to articulate what you need to be offered that would be better than what you currently have temping—a high salary, keeping your own hours, no anxiety, and downtime to work on your own projects. How much is this worth to you? We all have a different answer. How much would you take in exchange for sitting in the same seat every week for the rest of the year? Pick a number. Now add 20 percent. That's a good place to start your salary negotiations.

Calling Your Agencies: Throttle Up

Once you've made the decision to go for it, call all the counselors at your different agencies. This even includes the ones you registered at a long time ago but rarely used. You're changing your status to "looking to go permanent" and this is a perfectly valid excuse to call an agent. As they say on the waterfront, "You can't get nibbles if you don't cast a line."

Find an agency that specializes in the field you're interested in. Or even better, find out which agencies the specific companies you're interested in use, then apply to them.

You may be able to earn more money per hour in some specialty temp areas, but don't be distracted. If you're looking for a job in broadcasting, you won't reach that end by spending your days at a law firm. You know ABC, NBC, CBS, and Fox all use temps, make yourself one of the ones on their short list. And always carry your resumé in fifteen variations.

However you go about it, begin spending your days at the companies you want to work for permanently. Make yourself indispensable, network, watch the bulletin boards for job postings, eavesdrop for opportunities, and learn to speak up. You're there for a reason.

Directly contact all the companies you want to work for and let them know you're interested in permanent or freelance work. At least it registers your name, and if it works out, you're on your way and don't need me anymore.

The Points to Consider

Temping at a company before joining with a full-time job allows you unique look-before-buying options that applicants going through the personnel office don't get. Enjoy them all liberally.

◆ *Culture:* This may be the most important. Is this a place where you'd like to spend most of your waking hours? Is it pleasant to be in or are you eager to leave? There's more on this in chapter 7. If you like to work to music but can hear a tissue rustle here—boogie on, reggae temp.

◆ *Coworkers:* Are these people you want to spend your life with? Are they friendly or aloof? Are they cliquey or trippy? Are they quiet and dour or sweet and sour? Do they come with a free soda or sesame noodles?

◆ *Boss:* Are your styles compatible? If you like to work independently and your supervisor is going to be sitting next to you, move. Does he have a sense of humor, or is he just a cent-sniffing Hoover?

◆ *Equipment and supplies: True Story Department:* When I was applying for a job at a New York newspaper, everything was looking great and they asked me back for a second interview. That was when I found out I'd be given a manual typewriter instead of a computer to work on! Holy freak show! Moral of the True Story: Always take stock of the stock stash before you talk cash. If you have to ask for a pen, you can't afford to work there.

◆ *Salary, raises, and advancement:* How frequently are raises and promotions given out? What would your title be? What would your *next* title be? Where's it going? *Is* it going?

◆ *Benefits and perks:* Does the company offer health benefits? Retirement plans? Stock options? How much vacation time? Sick and personal days? What are the other perks? You're allowed to ask. It's okay.

Make them sell the job to you. If they don't have visible pride and confidence doing this, there's something wrong.

It's a complex combination of tangibles and intangibles that determines whether you leap out of bed in the morning or stay curled up under the covers in denial of the daylight. Confucius say, "Choose a job you love, and you will never have to work a day in your life." I say, "If your stomach's in knots on Sunday night, you're headed in the wrong direction on Monday morning."

Just as marriage won't fix the problems you had while dating, you won't resolve your grievances simply by going full-time. Iron out your differences while you still want each other and before you fall into a daily routine.

Ask every question you can think of in the beginning because it's a lot easier to say no before you've said yes.

Gainfully Employed at The Wright Place, Inc.

Let's say you've been out cruising in Temp Town for a while and you've finally found Mr. Wright, Inc., fallen in love, and now want to move in. Could happen.

Make yourself indispensable. Be the one the other workers come to with their computer questions. Or pick any field of specialty. Be the one who knows how to get a messenger service to really rush a package. Devise more efficient systems than are currently being used and quietly implement them. Share your knowledge, always hinting there's a lot more where that came from.

Blend in. If you seem as though you've always been there, they'll figure you always will be. If you're a member of the team and you share in other people's projects, no one will want you to leave.

Drug Testing vs. Testing Drugs

Although more and more companies are testing for drugs, tons and tons still aren't. If you're considering vital public safety professions such as, say, bank teller, you should probably lay off the smack, at least while you're applying.

If you've got a problem with drug testing, you may have a bigger problem than drug testing. If you're currently in your drug phase, you may want to hold off applying for that serious career position until it runs its course. You can't play in the pro leagues if you're still sucking on a security blanket. Besides, if you're honestly using drugs that the company you're applying to doesn't approve of, you're probably not going to fit in. You need only consider that famous Temp Commandment outtake from the *Let It Be* sessions: "If you can't pass the drug test, you don't want to work there anyway."

But there is a disclaimer: Even though most Republicans and

other single-cell protozoa invite Philip Morris and Jim Beam on every picnic while tossing all other drugs in the same minimum-jail-sentence basket, personnel supervisors understand the difference between marijuana and cocaine. If everyone in America who smoked a joint was fired, there wouldn't be enough people left to feed Newt Gingrich breakfast.

True Story Department

A person was recently being considered for an executive position at one of America's leading corporations, and it was discovered he had a criminal record for possessing two grams of marijuana in Texas. When the corporate head of personnel was asked about it on a conference call, he said, "Hell, the fatties I twist on the weekend are twice as big as that!"

He got the six-figure job.

THC, the active ingredient in marijuana, hash, and your better margarita mix, is not considered an automatic disqualification in all fields that test for drugs. In fact, Jimmy Carter, George Schultz, William F. Buckley Jr., Ken Kesey, Paul Krassner, Willie Nelson, Woody Harrelson, and a cloud of others are pushing to legalize it, but until that happens, we all have to say something like we "didn't inhale" so people will know we're telling the truth and to meet us behind the garage in five minutes. I only mention this because I'm trying to pad the book out and not because I endorse psychedelic epiphanies on the beach at dawn or anything.

Let's Review

Take the lump-in-the-throat test to make sure going permanent is really the move you want to make; understand your own require-ments and clearly lay them out to your prospective employer; apply directly to the companies you want to work for as well as the agencies that service them; tell your counselors what you're looking for; keep making money temping while you gather more experience and chart new directions; always carry a copy of your resumé and the file on a disk so you can customize it at the job if necessary; use the training missions to your various jobsites to prepare yourself in every way for when you get your real gig; take your time and don't accept less than your dream; take time off from your training to walk in the park and imagine your grand vision so you'll clearly know what you're looking for—and will be quick as a computer command when you see it.

14

-Landing a Job in a Day-

Let's say you've been temping and looking for a full-time job for a long time but never really found the exact match for your paisley pants until all of a sudden you're sent on a one-day assignment to a new place and realize the minute you walk in the door that you want to live there forever.

Only problem is, it's not your house—yet. You're faced with the nearly impossible task of trying to turn that around in the next eight hours. This is one of the hardest tricks to turn in all the hallowed halls of Career Search U., but now, thanks to a revolutionary new process developed by Italian scientists working on speech acceleration experiments in New York City, they have perfected the Score-a-Job-in-a-Day Theory of Relatively Difficult Things to Do. And since we have been together so long, dear reader, I'd be remiss in not sharing this rapid-deployment procedure that should be attempted only by qualified professionals who are pretty darn sure they want a full-time job.

Here's how:

Let's say at 8 A.M. you get a call to go in on a one-day assignment to a company you think you might like to work for. Bring your portfolio if applicable, and your resumé on paper and diskette.

When you arrive at 9:00, begin a methodical step-by-step procedure of evaluating every ramification of working there and let's say by 9:01 you've come to the positive conclusion that you want to spend the rest of your life there. By 9:03 you've already fantasized about the executive offices with a view so that by 9:05 you've come back to the hallway on earth, and now you'd like me to hurry up and get to the point because this is really *really* important, okay?

Alright, Bucko, buckle your seat belt. Here goes.

Careers in Eight

First and foremost do your job really well and don't screw around, because you have just met your Golden Goose. You want to treat her right from the moment that 9:01 bell goes off in your head. Meet, greet, and be real sweet. Review the chapter on acing the first day, although if you have to do that at this point you probably aren't going to get the job anyway. I assume you've run a few laps by now and you're one lean, mean, temping machine and the basics are something you could do while simultaneously solving *pi*.

Next, secretly start gathering data and friends and talking to secretaries and other people about working there. Ask the following questions: What's it like working here? Would you recommend it? How long have you been here? Do you know if anybody's leaving? Are any other departments looking right now? This seems nice on the outside but is it really once you're here? Is there much turnover? What kind of experience or type of person are they looking for? Do they have good health benefits? Did you come here through an agency or an ad or how?

Remember: Polite, honest, and straightforward talk. If you want to work there, be up front about it. Most people aren't. You may never be back to this place again. And now, after surveying all the people you can find, you've only got seven hours left!

Start sorting the mail. Start doing the work. Start bonding with your golden Mother Goose.

One for the money, use every trick. Two for the show, grab the phone quick. Three to get ready, type everything fast. And four to go forward so you don't finish last.

Quick—read the office manual. Heck, *copy* the office manual. Copy the phone sheet. Memorize what you can. Write down the drive and file directories. Figure them out. Gather data. Prepare your Letterhead Tip Sheet right away. Consolidate notes. Begin a *Mission Impossible* Secret Dossier Folder—because now there's less than six hours left!

In the first quiet moment call your counselor and tell her you'd like to go long-term or perm. "Are they looking for permanent people here? How long have they been a client? How often do you send people here? What's the personnel supervisor like?" Tell her you love her. Tell her you need her. Tell her it'll never be anyone else but her, because now it's nearly lunchtime and you've got less than five hours left!

Quick, scamper down to personnel to learn the route. Go in politely to ask what the lunch policy is for temps, but you're really performing a visual vibe reconnaissance of all data and body language for future analysis. Be friendly and nice, not small-talking and flighty. PHAST, I'm telling you, PHAST.

Just before you leave, say, "Hey, this is a real nice place to work," and make a quick eye-contact, burn-it-in parting smile, but not waiting for a response, just flash that knowing power-nod of nice-to-meet-you-and-we'll-meet-again-old-friend kind of nodding smile, because now you've got less than four hours left!

If there are any phone calls you have to make, use a pay phone and be quick about it. Make all personal calls on the outside. Don't jeopardize your time inside for a single minute. Skip lunch if you can, or eat light and eat fast. Take a small, no-mess snack back to your desk or wolf something quickly outside without spilling anything and double-check yourself before you go back in, which you'd better do quickly because this may be the most important time to be at your desk. This is the one downtime quiet hour when people might give you their inside personal tip or trick secrets for working there. The office is cleared of the Snitches and rid of the bitches and people are just standing around silent in the skyscraper wilderness willing to talk to you. It's Make Friends Time. Ask if there's an opening. Be nice. But ask. It means you're showing interest. Ask. Talk to them, and you'd better do it now—because there's less than three hours left!

Watch for the next opening of quietness around Mother Goose's nest so you can quickly retrace the route to the personnel supervisor's office. Somewhere during the lunch hour, probably when you were out, personnel called Ms. Goose as well as the secretary nearest you and took their reports. If you've pulled off a Radar O'day as per instructions, we're looking at two thumbs up from Siskel and Goose. Shortly after this, and while personnel's still in a good mood from lunch, begin your chance-meeting walks past her door to catch her eye. If this doesn't work naturally after one or two flights, you just swoop right in there, 'cause now there's less than two hours left!

PHAST, think PHAST, that's what they like. You're a pro so time to let 'em know. "I've been working for years as a temp, including for some of the nicest, and nastiest, people in town, but there's a really positive feeling about this place. I really liked all the people I met and I'd love to work here some more." If this is the truth, it'll come through in your voice. If you're sure, if you're polite, honest, and straightforward, if you did everything right at your desk, if you're backed by a thumbs-up from Mother freakin' Goose for God's sake, you're going to have the job if it's there to be had and you can cook my gander if this don't hatch. Follow her lead, keep pushing yourself, but the big cash boulder should already be tumbling into your pocketbook.

Just in case the personnel person turns out to be a Witchwoman With a Problem, you can always use your triple-A-Team card and switch to Emergency Backup Plan B, because now you're down to one hour left!

Calmly shifting into Less-Than-One-but-More-Than-None mode, write your name and agency on a blank Rolodex card along with a nice little yellow Post-it note to the secretary you replaced saying how great everything went and how it would be nice to come back and do it again.

Now it's time to capitalize on your having been the most perfect, attentive, alert, nonobtrusive, helpful assistant Mother Goose ever had. You've made her love you even if voodoo Witchwoman doesn't, and so, my good reader who I am about to lose forever to the ranks of the employed, make a real special goodbye to Queen Mother Goose, handing her your card and saying, "If you ever need another temp, ask for me by name or you never know what you'll get," and smile real sweet. And she goes, "HONK! Honk! You're Honk! right."

An eye-contact freeze-frame, a leprechaun's twinkle, half a Japanese bow, and you bid farewell after finessing the work of all the king's horses and all the king's men—and laying the foundation to come back here again.

Let's Rock

Heigh diddle, diddle, the cat and the fiddle, the cow jumped over the moon; the little dog laughed to see such sport, and the dish ran away with the spoon.

Good luck. Be honest. Work hard.

15

-Staying Happy for the Rest of Your Life-

Find someone you love, and be really nice to them forever.

The Temp Commandments

1 *You're just a temp.*
2 *The work does not come to you: You must go to it.*
3 *This is a business of relationships.*
4 *Leave no trail.*
5 *Being a good person is the most important thing.*
6 *It's not the journey, it's how many pictures you take.*
7 *Be in love with your own life.*
8 *Laugh every night before sleep.*
9 *Like a doctor, be forever to your art on call.*
10 *There is only hope, hard work and you.*

-Appendix: The Richie Cunningham School of Do-Rightness-

Health Care

If you live in any civilized nation on earth, such as Canada, you can skip this entire chapter because you've already got health care. In fact, you can go back and read the milking the cows chapter again. But if you're stuck in the free country that costs more than any other, we Americans will be swimming through this goop for the rest of our lives.

The truth about health care is that to stay healthy you should exercise, take your vitamins, take the stairs, take your bike, take it easy, don't smoke tobacco, don't drink more than you have to, don't pick fistfights with people bigger than you, don't play contact sports after puberty, and don't get hit by a car.

Rick Danko, the bass player of The Band, put it this way: "Getting healthy is getting up in the morning instead of going to bed in the morning."

A shaman I met said she hadn't been to a hospital except to visit other people since she was born. I've lived that way ever since.

The human body is the most amazing invention in our immediate galaxy. It mostly fixes itself. If there's something wrong with you and you go to a doctor, nine times out of ten they tell you you'll be okay, then they give you an expensive prescription which alleviates a little bit of pain, and you go back home telling your brain that you're okay and your immune system cures you.

My technique is to skip the doctor in the prior sequence and go straight to the immune system with a chicken soup appetizer, orange juice, toast on the side, then maybe some vitamins, ginseng, acidophilus, and bedtime with cable.

On the off chance that something does happen to you, there are still walk-in or free clinics in every major city in America. If you have a serious injury—let's say you fall down a flight of stairs and break something—then go to the emergency room of the hospital in town that takes street people. All cities have what are called "public" hospitals which seem perfectly normal from the outside but are the places where people who can't pay are taken. (Find this out in advance.) (Like today.) (Write it down.)

When you go in, you'll be treated, given a hospital identification card, and allowed to return for follow-up treatment on whatever you were first brought into the emergency room for. Poor people are designed into the system. Hospitals are set up to handle patients, and once you're in there the doctors don't know whether you're a Rockefeller or that Rascal feller.

Another option is to save your money from whatever health insurance program you might consider and just keep a mental note of it. An average U.S. health insurance plan will charge its members around $225 a month, which comes to $2,700 a year for the freedom to get sick. This is of course with a huge deductible, and would only cover a certain percentage of your bills anyway because even with so-called "insurance" you still end up paying for a huge chunk of your bills yourself.

As an example, since starting temping fifteen years ago, by not making the yearly $2,700 charity donation to the White-Coat Paper Pusher Fund, I've spent over $40,000 in health insurance premiums on better things. I'd have to get sick to a tune of more than forty grand worth of the expenses *they would cover* before insurance would have even paid for itself.

The Industrial Medical Complex

The Industrial Medical Complex makes the military look like a cost-efficient good idea. If you think the underground drug trade is corrupt and dangerous, the protected monopolies of the FDA drug manufacturers make the Cali Cartel look like bake sale matrons. Ever wonder why the American Medical Association voted without debate against doctor-assisted suicides or ending the life of terminally ill patients? Ever wonder why your government allows cigarettes to be sold virtually unregulated at prices children can afford, but nicotine gum or the patch cost $100 a hit and until recently required paying off a doctor for a prescription to allow you to quit? Ever wonder why a tiny amount of medicine with hardly enough of the active ingredient to cure a mouse is so expensive? Ever wonder why you have to get every prescription filled out by a billable doctor? Ever wonder why the drugs that require a doctor's prescription in this country are sold over the counter for a third the price in every other civilized nation? Ever wonder why America's the only industrialized nation without any form of national health care program? No, it's a perfectly honorable profession. Doctors and the senators hiding in their closets really have nothing but your absolute best health paramount in their mind.

If I haven't convinced you to rely on your own body to heal you, which it can do better than any fleet of doctors, and you'd like to make a monthly contribution to their vacation fund, I'll outline a few insurance programs that will gladly accept your money and even pay upward of 2 percent of any subsequent medical bills you may receive.

Comparing Health Plans

Since most of you are used to getting your health coverage first through your parents, then your schools, then your full-time regular employers, you're probably unsure about how to get health insurance on your own. In fact, hey-hey—it's easy!

Step One

Most temp agencies now offer an affiliated health care program that you may be eligible for after your first assignment, or after six months with the agency, or some variation of same. Ask your agency to mail you their packet. If your agency doesn't offer a reasonable (or any) health care program, call other agencies. Over half of all reputable temp agencies now offer some form of health coverage.

Step Two

Call the large national organizations and ask them to mail you their membership policy information packets. Just grab your Yellow Pages and flip to "Health—Maintenance Organizations" and let your fingers do the riffing.

Step Three

Since the different enrollment packages will arrive at staggered times, do the following survey as each comes through your mail slot. Using a separate blank pad for each, write out the following criteria for each company, plus your own personal additions. By evaluating each company with the same questions in the same order on separate pads, it's easy to condense the complex brochures and legalese into a readable summary you can assess. Make up your own comparative criteria, but here are some of the important factors:

Premiums per month, per year: It's a fair question to ask the provider for their premium history for the last few years so you can evaluate how quickly and by how much they're raising their rates per year.

Deductible per claim: The lower the deductible, the higher the premiums. The higher the deductible, the lower the premiums.

Percentage of costs covered: Eighty percent coverage or

above is the industry standard and you should consider nothing lower.

Coverage: Does it cover the things you're going to need?
Some programs are not good for children and other
living things. Others do offer prenatal, postnatal, and
day care. If you won't require these types of services,
for instance, then smaller, less expensive programs
may be open to you.

Maximum coverage: The minimum to accept here is $1
million, and you better not get sicker than that or your
mother's going to have a fit.

Renewability: You want to see the word "noncancelable."
If you don't, you can pretty much expect them to
abandon you at the exact moment you need them.

Stop-loss amount: This means the amount up to which
point you must pay part of; over that amount you
don't have to pay anything. It usually reads "100
percent after $10,000," which means they pay the
total bills over the amount of $10,000, but you split all
costs below that.

By writing these out on separate pads you should be able to
clearly scan across them and see who's the best for you. If you need
more help, you can call the government's Agency for Health Care
Policy and Research at 800-358-9295, and ask them for their very
useful and easy-to-read booklet, "Checkup on Health Insurance
Choices."

If you want another nonbiased opinion, you can contact the
National Women's Health Network at 202-347-1140. They're kind
of the Greenpeace of the medical world, and if they recommend a
plan you know it's going to be ethical and human-friendly.

Once you complete the above evaluation, you'll see how little
that permanent full-time job was really worth. Now you can have all
the same health benefits you thought were so priceless in that
prison sentence you called your job.

Medicare, Medicaid, and HMOs

Medicare

This is for people over 65 or disabled, hence the "care." It's run by the federal government, so it's unbelievably complicated and huge. It's probably not going to be around in another week so there's no sense reading too much about it. If you're on Social Security, you're already on it, and probably on top of it. It's not something that affects many temps, and if you are eligible for it, you're probably not reading this book to learn more about it so we'll just move right along.

Medicaid

This is for low-income people, as in Student Aid, Financial Aid, or Medic Aid. Although financed by the federal government, it's bob doled out to each state, which makes its own determination as to who is eligible. Look in the state government pages of your local phone book for the Medicaid Program information number and they'll send you the eligibility information and application. If you think you may be eligible and want to get a simple overview, you can get a free copy of the government's "Medicaid Fact Sheet" by writing to: Health Care Financing Administration, Office of Public Affairs, Room 403B, Hubert H. Humphrey Building, 200 Independence Avenue, S.W., Washington, DC 20201.

Health Maintenance Organization (HMO)

With the health care debate raging in the national media for the last few years, you have undoubtedly heard the term "HMO," which stands for "Health Maintenance Organization," or "Heathens Milking Others," depending on your point of view. These are like big clubs that subsidize your visits to the doctor. They cost between $200 and $400 a month to be a member. Most offer what *are called "copayments," where you pay a nominal fee ($5–$25) for each service that you use, and they pay the remainder. This arrangement will apply to everything from ambulance fees to emergency room visits to physical therapy.*

There's a wide variance in national HMO coverage, but many are fairly supportive of preventative care such as regular physicals, pre- and postnatal care, immunizations, and mammograms. Many are now covering mental health doctors and offering discount memberships at health clubs.

Another reason HMOs are popular is because the costs are fixed so there are (supposedly) no surprises. Also, you don't have to fill out forms for every little thing you do: you just present a member card when you see the doctor and the HMO sends you a bill for the nominal copayment amount. Once you pay that, they pay the remainder.

The most common complaint about HMOs is that you have to use their doctors. But they've got lists as thick as telephone books and almost all doctors participate in some HMO. They're usually affiliated with one particular hospital in your area. If you have a doctor you really like and aren't willing to change, these plans might not be for you.

The second most common complaint is that HMOs are denying patients care in order to cut costs. Do a diligent evaluation of the performance record of the local HMO you're considering. Ask people you know until you find someone who's a member. Get firsthand information. Follow your local news for stories of fraud or mismanagement. Check the Better Business Bureau report. I'm not sure, but I think most HMOs have been taken over by the Saving & Loan guys, so it's always Patient Beware month in the land of medicine.

Here's one cool option that probably won't be in your phone book but is in fact managed by the National Association of Temporary Services:

National Association of Temporary and Staffing Services
Group Health Insurance
119 South Saint Asaph Street
Alexandria, VA 22314
Insurance questions: TempMed 800-323-2106

The advantage of this plan is that it can be bought in segments of 30 to 180 days, and you can carry it with you from agency to agency.

Or you can call the very hip Alternative Health Group which offers different inexpensive plans in most states. You can pick any doctor or hospital, and they offer coverage for holistic, naturopathy, bodywork, chiropractic, midwives, and preventative care.

The Alternative Health Group
P.O. Box 6279
Thousand Oaks, CA 91359-6279
800-966-8467

Coverage Through Preexisting Organizations

There are so many health care collectives out there today that almost any group, church, club, organization, association, school, or long-distance company has a health care program you can join.

- ◆ If your spouse or parents have health care, your least expensive route is probably being added to their policy if you're eligible. Ask around the house.
- ◆ Call your credit card companies; many are affiliated with some form of health insurance program. You can request details by calling the 800 number listed on your bills.
- ◆ You may already be eligible through an organization or association you belong to. Call them up. If you're not a member of a social or business group but are considering joining, now may be worth it because of the added bonus

191

of acquiring inexpensive health care along with the other benefits that made you consider joining in the first place. For instance, the Screen Actor's Guild (SAG) provides *free* medical and hospital benefits to all members who earn more than $7,500 per year in acting salaries, and free dental and life insurance to members earning more than $15,000 a year.

And if none of the above work, you can always move to Canada.

Inexpensive Dental Coverage

Both large and small cooperative dental plans have sprung up in the last decade and are operating all over the country. Call the ones in your Yellow Pages and ask them to mail you rate schedules (their names contain words like "Dental Group"). Anybody can join—you don't have to be part of any company or corporation. They have the same or better prices than most company's affiliated dental plans, the membership fees range from $50 to $150 a year, and you can switch dentists if you don't like the one you're seeing.

Here are two of the best and cheapest in the country:

Signature Dental Plan
200 N. Martingale Road
Schaumberg, IL 60173-2096
800-346-0310

National plan, reasonable rates. Anybody can join.

Northeast Dental Plan of America
845 Third Avenue
New York, NY 10022
800-828-2222

Inexpensive, but only available in the Northeast

Most towns have at least one university with a dental program where you can join and be a human guinea pig for a fraction of the cost of regular dental care. Many offer really good care, sometimes better than going to old dentists who still use baking soda and shoelaces, but you also might get Hans Klutz who starts shaking at the sight of saliva and jabs a needle through your cheek. Your call.

The best dental plan is to brush your teeth after meals and before going to sleep using an American Dental Association–approved toothpaste. In fact, if you don't see ADA ACCEPTED on a dental product, don't buy it.

Always carry a toothbrush with you whenever you leave the house for longer than a grocery run, as well as a minitube of toothpaste (or the end of an old one rolled tight for those last minute road splashes of fresh paste), and some bubble-gum-flavored dental floss. Use them. Don't eat much chocolate or sugary goo stuff, floss more than occasionally, use Listerine after brushing to kill germs because that's what rots your teeth, and try one of those new electric toothbrushes. If you haven't driven a Braun lately, you haven't gone electric.

Financial Planning

Temping is like retirement in that you're no longer scurrying along in the gutters of the rat race. You have lots of time to do whatever you want, you're not under some superior's thumb, you don't have to take the same route to sit in the same seat week after week, and you've already got a gold watch to remind you how much free time you've got!

If, while you're practicing for all the fun you'll have later in life, you'd also like to train your money to make money in a tax-free interest-bearing account, you may want to consider some form of a retirement plan. Along with no health care, the loss that temps most frequently lament is the fat company-subsidized retirement plan. Retirement may seem like Pluto when you're temping on Earth, but there are lots of numerical benefits to laying your nest egg before the future gets any closer.

Planning Your Future

The first step is having a financial goal with concrete numbers. Remember "The Ongoing Expense Report" in chapter 11? You need to apply that same accurate, hard-number philosophy to the cash flow of your future. If you live to be 85, and you retire at age 60, you'll have to support yourself—maybe alone—for twenty-five years.

The second step is understanding your personal finances so you can plan your expenses. Some personal variables to assess are your current expenses (the bottom line of your "Ongoing Expense Report") and expectation of future expenses—whether you'll have a mortgage or not, whether you're paying for college for the kids, or will you be the primary caretaker for a loved one? These and other uplifting fiscal questions must be answered before you can begin to take care of them.

The third step is formulating a plan to meet these goals. Having a plan to follow is more important than which particular plan you choose. Every financial planner will tell you that people who implement a specific plan to achieve a specific goal are much more likely to reach financial independence than those who just save without a plan.

Forever Young

It's never too late to start saving, and it's never too early. In fact, the quicker you start, the easier it is to get rich. If you only invest $10,000 toward retirement, will you earn more if you invest it when you're 45 or 25? If you can put away a little money when you're young, then leave it untouched for years, it'll just keep multiplying over and over until you retire. Can you imagine?

If a twenty-five-year-old invests $2,000 a year for ten years earning 6 percent per year, compounded monthly, and then never invests anything else until retirement, she'll have $225,000 to retire on. If a thirty-five-year-old invests the same $2,000 a year for ten years, she'll have $100,000 at retirement. Big difference. Investing the same amount ten years earlier means *more than double* the money.

The End: Spouses, Pensions, and Social Security

Social Security—if it still exists by the time you read this—will not pay enough to keep your pet alive. It's estimated that as soon as

2005, Social Security will only make up 18 percent of the money retirees live on! And it's even harder for most women to survive on Social Security since their social security benefits average only 65 percent of a male counterpart's because of work descriptions and patterns and the fact that men have been running Washington for far too long.

The balance of the money that most retirees live on is a combination of personal savings, pensions, long-term retirement accounts, unearned income (for example, rent you earn from property you lease), and earned income (for example, retirees working at jobs like temping to make ends meet).

Sometimes this is easier to prepare for if you're married, although I don't recommend it. Especially not for the money. But if you're married and your spouse has a job, perhaps even a full-time job with a pension plan, find out the details. Not only will it help you to know how much you should be saving to fairly contribute, it's important to find out that information while you can; should your spouse die unexpectedly, you don't want to be learning about his or her finances for the first time at the same time you're grieving.

Don't take it for granted that you'll have a spouse to help you with expenses in retirement, especially if you're a woman. Eighty-five percent of women have to take charge of their own finances at some point in their lives. The high divorce rate and the shorter lifespan of men (there's a two to three ratio of men to women over the age of 50) means that most women will have to face their later years alone. Plan for it and you won't be disappointed.

An increasingly common type of long-term retirement savings plan that companies offer their employees are 401k plans. Some temp agencies are now offering them, so ask your counselor. You have to leave your money tied up for years, but they pay off at the finish line.

Cool Option for Undisciplined Savers

This is an option that financial ledgerheads would never endorse, so naturally I gravitated right to it. If you're one of those people who can't seem to save any money, try this diet:

On the federal W-4 wage and tax form at your agency, in the Dependents' box, write the number zero so it's like you have no children or spouse, a freedom the government charges you a premium for by taking more taxes out. But also, look at Line 6. It says, "Additional amount, if any, you want withheld from each paycheck." You can write in whatever dollar amount you'd like to have the government withhold each pay period. Note: This can be revised upward or downward at any time.

Right now I'm sure you have zero on that line. Have your agency mail you a new W-4 form and change the amount. Mail it back in and then all future checks will be debited the amount you specified.

"Yeah right, give the government more money in taxes?"

Not quite. You're just having them hold onto it so you won't spend it; it's still yours and you'll get it all back at tax time.

The reason ledgerheads hate this is because Uncle Sam earns the interest on your money during the year and doesn't bother to pass it on to you. Of course it would be wiser to put the extra money into a healthy tax-deferred account instead of "lending" it to the government. But if you don't have the capital or are not disciplined enough to do this, the W-4 trick is the surest way to have extra money at tax time. When you receive the big fat check at the start of the next year, you can put all the money you never missed straight into some sort of tax-free IRA. Or you can buy yourself something better than lunch.

Let's Review One Last Time

Heal yourself; live long and prosper; diversify your savings; never bet more than you can lose; always tell the truth; follow your bliss, and leave nothing but footprints.

-Appendix: Official Places and Secret Numbers-

Here are some organizations that might help make the journey more enlightening, entertaining, profitable and easy to navigate.

Please explore the universe freely.

The Alternative Health Group
P.O. Box 6279
Thousand Oaks, CA 91359-6279
800-966-8467
Hip holistic health care.

American Automobile Association (AAA)
800-789-7391
Not-for-profit, great benefits, going places.

America Online
800-827-6364
If you're not online yet, this is the easiest way.
Tell them Karmacoupe sent ya.

Attorney General Janet Reno
Constitution and 10 Street, N.W.
Washington, DC 20530
202-633-2000
In case anybody gives you a hard time.

Buddha Books
Society for Buddhist Understanding
16925 E. Gale Avenue
City of Industry, CA 91745
818-961-9661
Write or call and you might get a book that'll solve all your problems.

Canadian Tourism
800-577-2266
Cool place to visit with all your spare money.

Central Park Visitor's Center
The Dairy
65 Street and the center of the park
Central Park
New York, NY 10021
See God in over eight hundred acres.

The Chelsea Hotel
222 West 23 Street
New York, NY 10011
212-243-3700
Really weird place to stay if you're ever in New York.

Department of Labor
200 Constitution Avenue, N.W.
Washington, DC 20210
202-523-9475
Check your local phone book for listings.

Environmental Protection Agency
401 M Street, S.W.
Washington, DC 20460
202-382-2090

Equal Employment Opportunity Commission
2401 E Street, N.W.
Washington, DC 20507
202-663-4264
Check your local phone book for office nearest you.

Federal Labor Relations Authority
500 C Street, S.W.
Washington, DC 20424
202-382-0711

The Grateful Dead
P.O. Box 1065
San Rafael, CA 94901
201-744-7700
415-457-6388
http://grateful.dead.net/
Excellent stress-relief medicine.

Health and Human Services Department
Executive Office Center
2101 East Jefferson Street
Suite 501
Rockville, MD 20852
800-358-9295
Ask for their "Checkup on Health Insurance Choices" booklet.

Health Care Financing Administration
Office of Public Affairs
Room 403B
Hubert H. Humphrey Building
200 Independence Avenue, S.W.
Washington, DC 20201
Provides free fact sheets on many subjects including Medicaid.

The Kettle of Fish Institute
130 West Third Street
New York, NY 10012
Personal interactive training, and darts.

Key-Z Productions
755 Polk Street
Eugene, OR 97402
541-484-4315
Instructional books and videos. Call or write for brochure.

Late Show With David Letterman
The Ed Sullivan Theater
1697 Broadway
New York, NY 10019
Ticket information: 212-975-1003
For some temporary fun, mail them a postcard and go see the show!

Metropolitan Museum of Art
Fifth Avenue and 82 Street
New York, NY 10028
212-535-7710
See God in over two thousand incarnations.

Museum of Television and Radio
25 West 52 Street
New York, NY 10019
212-621-6600
Good place to research the many TV shows referenced throughout
this book.

The National Arbor Day Foundation
Nebraska City, NE 68410
They send you ten free real live trees as soon as you join! Write for
information.

The National Association of Temporary Services
119 South Saint Asaph Street
Alexandria, VA 22314-3119
703-546-6287
http://www.natss.com/staffing/
For health insurance questions call: 800-232-2106

The National Foundation for the Arts
1100 Pennsylvania Avenue, N.W.
Washington, DC 20506
202-682-5400
This is the "endowment." Write for a grant application.

The National Organization for Women (NOW)
1000 16 Street, NW
Washington, DC 20036-5705
The future of the world lies in your hands. Check your phone book
for your local chapter.

The National Women's Health Network
1325 G Street, N.W.
Washington, DC 20005
202-347-1140

The National Writers Union
873 Broadway, Suite 203
New York, NY 10003-1209
212-254-0279

The Occupational Safety and Health Review Commission
1925 K Street, N.W.
Washington, DC 20006

The Public Citizen Health Research Group
2000 P Street, N.W.
Washington, DC 20036
202-833-3000

Reliable Office Supply
800-735-4000
They'll UPS you office supplies for $3 an order. You can order as little as $5 worth.

Rollerblades
800-232-7655
After sex, one of the best ways to stay in shape.

The Sierra Club
85 Second Street
San Francisco, CA 94105-3441
415-997-5500
Since temps live on earth, we need to have one in order to work. I've been a member for years and haven't been sick a day in my life, plus they mail you their nature magazine that makes *National Geographic* look like a business journal. Check your phone book for a local chapter.

SecretAgent Sandy
Your New Agency
212-697-8367

Small Business Administration
1441 L Street, N.W.
Washington, DC 20416
202-653-6554

The White House
1600 Pennsylvania Avenue
Washington, DC 20500
202-456-1414
202-456-2461 (fax)
President@whitehouse.gov

Yoko Ono
Instant Karma, Inc.
1 West 72 Street
New York, NY 10023
Could be one of those weird addresses you need one day, and
boom, here it is!

Zip Code Information
800-522-9085
You give them an address, they tell you a zip code. Free! If that
number doesn't work in your state, look up the "Postal Business
Center" in the government pages of your local phone book. All
major cities have one, and they have a CD-ROM of all addresses in
the United States and can give you the number in a digital second.

Tempheads Unite!

• • • •

Who are you? Where are you? How are you?

My wave on the surfboard is **TempNation@aol.com**

Let me know how it's going!

• • • •

-Index-

205